THE SINBUSTER of SMOKY BURN

THE SINBUSTER of SMOKY BURN

The Memoirs
of a Student Minister
on the Prairies

HUGH W. McKERVILL

WHITECAP BOOKS
Vancouver / Toronto

WOOD LAKE BOOKS
Winfield

Published simultaneously by Wood Lake Books Inc.,
Box 700, Winfield, BC, V0M 2C0

Edited by Iain MacDonald
Cover design by Warren Clark
Interior design by Susan Doering
Typography by CryptoGraphics, Vancouver, BC

Second Printing, 1994

Printed and bound in Canada by D.W. Friesen and Sons Ltd.,
Altona, Manitoba

Canadian Cataloguing in Publication Data

McKervill, Hugh W.
Sinbuster of Smoky Burn

ISBN 1-55110-096-7 (Whitecap Books)
ISBN 0-929032-99-3 (Wood Lake Books)
1. McKervill, Hugh W. 2. United Church of Canada—Clergy—
Biography. 3. Rural clergy—Prairie Provinces—Biography. I. Title.
BX9883.M244A3 1993   287.92'092   C93-091535-6

The publisher acknowledges the assistance of the Canada Council
in making this publication possible.

Acknowledgements

This book is the result of many people helping me along the way.

Quite a few people with special expertise kindly provided or verified data, making the factual matter more accurate than it might have been.

The good folk of Battle Heights, Smoky Burn, and Papikwan were enthusiastic in their support and participation. Their personal recollections, and their generous sharing of treasured photographs, added authenticity to the historical dimension of the story.

My dear friends Gray and Eleanor Campbell have shown so much faith in me over the years. Were it not for their encouragement I might not have ventured again so hopefully into the realm of authorship.

Finally, without the astute counsel of Iain MacDonald, my editor, the story would not have emerged in its present format.

Thank you all for helping make this book come into being.

Introduction

This is a true story. It is a recollection of personal experiences and observations from a period of history almost forty years ago. Much as I would like to think otherwise, I realize that my memory, even when nourished with notes from yesteryear, is less than perfect. Therefore, in an effort to ensure authenticity I have consulted experts, reviewed documentation, and interviewed many of the people mentioned in these pages. They are, after all, the real authorities.

While I have attempted to ensure that important details are correct, this story makes no claim to be an exhaustive, factual report. If I had wanted to write a treatise I would have applied to the Canada Council for a grant, or I might have registered in a Ph.D. program in history. That way I wouldn't have to worry about many people actually reading the thing. More significantly, the final product would not have been "truthful." It might have been "fact-full," but that, in my opinion, is something altogether different.

For a true "story" to come to life, an elixir must be added to the drab matter of fact. Imagination! This is the raconteur's alchemy. If it works well, the storyteller can't quite account for the outcome.

There is one place where I have deliberately changed a fact. The tale of the truck ride from Carrot River to Battle Heights really happened, except that the driver of the Fargo truck was its owner, Barney Thiessen, not the character called Bob. Bob McKay did drive Barney's truck on occasion, and I did have a couple of scary rides with him. Barney's vocabulary and habits were more refined than Bob's. Imagination dictated that Bob should be the driver in the story.

Many years passed before I was able to write this book. I could have dug out data and dashed off a dissertation at college shortly after leaving the northern frontier. However, the story as told here could not have been written at that time, for it was necessary that the various elements should age and mature in the cellars of the soul before being decanted. I myself, am one of the elements.

During the period covered in this story Canada used the imperial system of measurements. I have, therefore, used imperial throughout.

A word about the title. Titles are tricky. They must be focused enough to capture the essence of the story while inviting broad interest, and they must do this in a few well-balanced words. Most of the events in this story relate to three communities: Battle Heights, Smoky Burn, and Papikwan. To have used all three names would have made the title a little too long.

It is my hope that this book honours the women and men who did the extraordinary work of opening up new territory in this part of the Canadian frontier. They were true builders of the nation, and I am proud to have been associated with them.

Contents

CHAPTER 1

Don't Forget Your Hat

It was the mid-fifties, the fabulous fifties, an era of energy and hope. The end of World War II was already a decade in the past. There was work to be had, and for those of us who were students at Canadian universities and colleges, there were summer jobs and the prospects of a career upon graduation. It was the spring of the year and I was in the springtime of life.

From the campus at Waterloo College I could gaze along the road leading off to Elmira. Recently stripped of snow and steaming in the new sun, it disappeared into the folds of western Ontario's winter-weary farmlands, luring me to far-away places, perhaps a backpacking trek through the Andes or maybe just a cherry Coke and a piece of raisin pie at an out-of-town diner. Overhead, Canada geese honked north, mocking my captivity. The temptation to pack a bag and simply take off was almost irresistible. On the other hand, fear of failure and all the horrors of that possible fate drove me to unprecedented levels of scholastic industry.

The whole rhythm of campus life had changed over the last couple of weeks. A mood of desperate seriousness had set in. The gymnasium, where one could usually thwart the strongest urge to study by whiling away an hour or two with a basketball, grew silent. Gone was the squeak of runners on hardwood and the thump, thump, thump of the ball. Only the sweaty odour lingered. Even the perpetual games of Bridge were discontinued and the density of tobacco smoke diminished in the common rooms. It was time for final examinations. The open road would have to wait.

It has always been part of the rites of spring in Canada that university examinations coincide with the first alluring overtures of warm weather. In the spring of 1955 I was a pre-theology student finishing my sophomore year in Arts and Science at Waterloo, and, like my peers, I was suffering the mixed pains of study fatigue and itchy feet. However, my restlessness was exacerbated by a letter which had just arrived from the headquarters of the United Church of Canada, announcing my appointment to a summer mission charge in northern Saskatchewan. Thus, stimulated by a prescient sense of adventure and inebriated with the sap of spring fever, it was all I could do to remain focused on studies. Fortunately for my eventual destiny, the need to gain a bachelor's degree for admission to theological studies won the battle of motivations.

As a form of internship in partial preparation for ordination, students for the ministry of the United Church of Canada were required to spend at least two summers in the service of the Board of Home Missions. Assignments were in parishes or communities where there was not enough money, interest, or neither, to pay the stipend of a full-time minister. To plug these perceived gaps in the spiritual coverage of the nation and, as I soon discovered, to test the mettle of her aspiring clerics, the Church employed a small army of theology and pre-theology students, and sent them forth each year "to serve." Notice of one's posting always arrived by mail at the height of final exams, when it would have the maximum unsettling effect.

Since most of the colleges were in the East, and the vast majority of summer mission charges were in the West, the risk of culture shock was substantial for all concerned. The Church's method of preparing the students and parishioners to cope with one another was profound in its simplicity. It was to do absolutely nothing. Equipped with the blessings of the Home Missions Board and little else, we fanned out into the remote corners of the nation, acting as ministerial as we could manage from April till September, at which time most of us returned to college. The experience was sufficient to put some fellows off the idea of a career in the Church for ever. The first year I signed up the pay was a hefty twenty-two dollars a week, plus keep, and, as the terms were explained to me, "Who knows, maybe more, if M. and M. (Missionary and Maintenance) givings are good this year."

Summer mission fields were usually in remote, sparsely populated regions. A few choice charges were to be found in tourist-infested locations in northern Ontario's holiday belt, and these were much sought after by some. But such locations held no attraction for me. I wanted challenge. Perhaps because I had grown up in the pastoral beauty of rural Northern Ireland I had developed a romantic, if unrealistic, attraction to the rugged Canadian West. Whatever the underlying reasons, I had made it known in my application that I was willing to go to a remote and difficult posting. When the letter of appointment arrived I began to realize I had been granted my request.

The arrival of these letters from the Home Missions Board stirred the little group of pre-theology students at Waterloo College into a state of considerable excitement. When we met in the cafeteria or the common room, or when we bumped into one another outside the library, letters were whipped out and exchanged for viewing. We compared locations, the number of preaching points, accommodation arrangements, and transportation. We speculated about what we might encounter and attempted to outdo one another with predictions of the difficulties we would have to overcome.

One or two of the more serious lads had a tendency to lurch into prayer, and the arrival of the letters sending us forth into the world was just too biblical for them to resist. Needless to say, I was not against prayer and spiritual devotion. Indeed, I had worked conscientiously at getting myself sufficiently righteous for the calling I was about to take on. For example, my vocabulary had undergone an amazing transformation since leaving the construction gangs where I had started apprenticing at age fifteen, and where I had worked as a journeyman carpenter before deciding to prepare for the ministry. A lot of the same words were employed, of course. They were simply intoned differently.

Likewise, my inner journey towards the decision to take up a life of service in the Church had been marked by much personal prayer. But I had never been comfortable with what I called "the sudden slump" approach, and at Waterloo I sometimes went to elaborate means to avoid a couple of the more unctuous members of the pre-theology group for fear that the mere mention of obtaining a good mark or landing a part-time job would evoke too much gratitude on my behalf and someone would say, "Let's have a word of prayer to give thanks."

When this happened everyone was expected to assume a slouching posture, head in hand, every eye closed, while one by one, with well-worn liturgical clichés and an occasional clever turn of phrase, each member of the group competed to demonstrate his unique level of intimacy with the Almighty.

My aversion to this ritual notwithstanding, one afternoon, between exams, I found myself part of a little group of fellow student missionaries who, having shared details of our respective assignments during a walk past the end of the football field, bowed our heads and gave thanks for what was about to happen to us.

What was to happen to me was set forth in terse instructions in my dimissory letter. I was to proceed to Carrot River, Saskatchewan, which was as far as the railway and gravel road went. Here I should contact my supervising pastor who would help me make my way to Battle Heights, Smoky Burn, and Papikwan.

The very sound of the place names made concentration on Spinoza, Voltaire, and Kant seem irrelevant. Yet, somehow the last exam was written. There were girls to kiss goodbye and vows of life-long companionship to pledge with fellows whose names I have long forgotten. The quartet in which I sang tenor rendered a few barber-shop numbers in our favourite music room. The urinals provided resonance. To the consternation of those still writing exams, our voices seeped into every quarter of the old, ivy-clad building by following pipes and heating ducts. I spent a weekend with my family amid the manicured lawns of London, Ontario and then, armed with two-thirds of a bachelor's degree, a Revised Standard Version of the Bible, a few books recommended by my own pastor to keep me on the theological straight and narrow, plus a brown fedora hat, I set out to subdue the West.

My father bought me the hat and it seemed destined to accompany me in spite of some efforts at forgetfulness on my part. I was blessed at that time with a thick head of hair and saw no practical need for a hat. Besides, there was the whole issue of self-image. I didn't see myself as a hat-bearing person. A cap, maybe. But a fedora? Yet, my father was a true Irish immigrant and knew better than I the authority a hat bestowed. He understood that it was the crown placed upon the head that signified the monarch's power, and that the bishop looked ineffectual without his mitre. You could not touch your hat to a passing lady unless you were actually wearing one, and it was essential to have it on your head in order to doff it with a flourish of humility upon entering the church sanctuary. Dad felt a hat would help me in my mission. It would bestow an element of dignity that might otherwise be missing in my bearing. So he bought his son a brown fedora with a discreet feather emerging from the narrow band.

My mother supported this purchase, though for purely maternal reasons.

"Now, don't forget your hat, Hugh," she reminded as I was gathering my belongings in preparation for departure.

"Yes, I've got it right here, Mum," I replied.

"You never know what the weather is going to be like away out there so you better make sure you've got it with you," she insisted.

"Yes Mum, I've got it ready to take along."

"Well, it's your business. If you end up catching your death of cold it will be your own fault."

"Mother. The hat's on my head. Look."

Later that day, with a tearful kiss from Mum and a meaningful hand clasp from Dad, I boarded the train from London to Toronto, where I would catch the "Continental" going west. The hat was part of my carry-on luggage.

CHAPTER 2

Mixed Train

U nder the clock in the cavernous atrium of Toronto Union
Station I met two classmates. They were also heading
west, but to charges in more settled, southern parts of
Saskatchewan and Alberta. We checked our tickets, looked
for the track number on the departures board, drank coffee at
the U-shaped counter in the station diner, and as soon as
boarding was permitted we lugged our suitcases along the
platform. Past the first-class lounge car we trudged, past the
first-class sleepers, past the dining car, exchanging nods of
greeting with proprietary porters, each standing beside the
step into his personal domain. The smell of metal, stale urine,
steam, coal dust, and smoke filled our nostrils—the perfume
of adventure—till at last we found our tourist sleepers, behind
the coach-class cars and the "head end" baggage and express
cars. Train No. 3, the "Continental Limited."

We dumped our bags and my hat on our respective seats,
which were in different cars, then met again on the platform so
we could walk forward and look at the engine, not realizing
that we were viewing a species on the brink of extinction.
Poised to pull a village of sixteen cars a distance of over 2,929
miles from Toronto to Vancouver, the "mountain type" steam
locomotive seethed like a mechanical leviathan. A ninety-foot
monster of mighty wheels and powerful shafts, of bulging
cylinders, pipes and pistons, it sighed hot fumes from its stack
and hissed steam from its joints. To feed it the tender carried
eighteen tons of coal and ten-thousand gallons of water. We

were in awe. There is nothing quite like a steam locomotive to a boy, even when the boy is a man, or is in the process of becoming one.

"Aaaaalla-board. Aaaaalla-board," the conductor's voice rolled along the platform, curling up at the end. We rushed to the nearest door and jumped in. The porter scooped up his step. At 11:00 P.M. the train lurched into motion. We were finished exams. We were on our way. We were on our way with our eastern college culture to the great Canadian West.

The three-day train trip from Toronto to Saskatoon was relatively uneventful. We visited the dining car a couple of times, but it was too expensive for our student pockets. Baked fillet of cod with cheese sauce was two dollars and seventy-five cents. A charcoal-broiled sirloin steak was completely out of range at four dollars and seventy-five cents. That was almost enough to pay my rent for a week where I roomed off campus. For thirty cents we could buy a pot of coffee, but the white-aproned steward was sullen at his prospects for a tip when we ordered a pot between the three of us. Cowed by his exaggerated display of service, we ordered raisin pie for another thirty cents each, and made the whole thing last a hundred miles.

At Capreol the Montreal and Toronto trains consolidated. We dashed to the station coffee shop and bought tasteless ham and cheese sandwiches that stuck to our teeth. The same at Hornepayne, by which time we were 723.8 miles from Toronto, the sign said.

My only other recollections seem to be associated with the smell of smoke and beer in the lounge car, and the difficulty of shaving in the men's washroom and smoker with its black, horse hair, leatherette bench, the brass spittoon on the floor in the corner circled by stains from thousands of miles of misses, and the water slurping out of the stainless steel sinks as the train lurched over the Canadian Shield and thundered onto the prairies.

At 8:45 on the evening of the third day, we pulled into Saskatoon. I bade farewell to my companions and found a room for the night at the Y.M.C.A. Early next morning I boarded Train No.32 heading north. It crawled cautiously across a flat, flooded landscape while rain whipped the coach windows and my spirits dampened commensurately.

Somewhere after one o'clock we reached the town of Melfort, where I was to change trains again for Carrot River. It was still raining and bitterly cold. The best information I could get from the taciturn station agent was that my connecting train would probably arrive in an hour or two. So, I found what comfort I could in the drab waiting room with its tongue-and-groove walls, blistered varnish, and the inevitable railway-lavatory smell. Time dragged. I read, dozed, paced the dingy waiting room, and read some more, but couldn't venture out because of the torrential rain.

After what seemed like an eternity in this solitary confine-ment, my spirits were encouraged by the sound of a train squealing to a stop. I grabbed my hat and suitcases and ran out into the deluge looking for the closest coach. All I could see was a long line of freight cars, several carrying livestock. "Wrong train," I thought, and beat a hasty retreat back into the waiting room. However, in a few minutes the station agent shoved his head through the doorway.

"You goin' to Carrot River, Mac?" He was dressed in oil-skins and a cascade of water ran off his hat.

"That's right," I replied. "How much longer do you think I'll have to wait?"

"Well," he said thoughtfully, wiping the back of his hand across his wet nose and mouth, "If you don't wanna get onto this one, I'd say there should be a train around about the day after tomorrow, though there's no telling with this here rain."

Throughout my solitary sojourn in Melfort railway station, the station agent had passed back and forth through the waiting room a few times on his way to carry out some arcane purpose. His replies to my various questions had been economical in the extreme. Whatever the question or attempt at conversation on my part the response had generally been a laconic, "Yep," or "Nope."

"Do you think the train to Carrot River will be along soon?"

"Yep."

"Is there a restaurant close by where I could get something to eat?"

"Nope."

"I'll get him," I thought. "Did you know that the toilet is broken and the washroom is flooded?"

"Yep," he replied without breaking stride, leaving me to wonder whether it was or not.

This demonstration of reticence was almost a pleasant change after the incessant flow of verbiage to which I had been subjected for the past months at college. However, I now felt an acute need for further information for, clearly, I had seen a freight train, not a passenger train, sitting at the platform. My perplexity must have shown. Breaking with his customary style only slightly the station agent condescended to explain.

"Passenger coach z'at the end of the train," he announced, with a jerk of his thumb over his shoulder in the direction he wanted me to go. "Mixed train." With that, he slid back into the wind and the rain.

Collar up, chin tucked in, left shoulder forward, I wedged my way along the platform against the wind and rain, past the cars of doleful cattle, past the shifting horses, towards—sure enough—a lone passenger car at the end of the train, well beyond the reach of the platform.

I climbed aboard and, pretending to be oblivious to the gapes of the few passengers already there, I found an empty seat and hoisted my dripping suitcases onto the overhead rack. Stoically, I maintained an air of nonchalance as a mini-cataract drained from the cases and ran down my neck. A whistle blew. The steam engine burst into a spasm of excited puffing, spinning its wheels on the wet tracks before settling down to a laborious pull. I thought of the cattle and horses up front as we jerked ahead. When the gaping in the coach relented I inconspicuously moved the dripping suitcases over the empty seat ahead and settled in for the last leg of the journey to Carrot River.

Canadian railways have a class system that operates geographically. The further away from the main line the more dilapidated the passenger facilities. This was a basic operational principle which, when carried to logical conclusion, would lead to the elimination of whole lines. The Monday, Wednesday, and Friday train from Saskatoon to Melfort had been noticeably less comfortable than the "Continental" from Toronto west. The coach I now boarded was a relic. In one corner stood a pot-bellied stove; beside it in a metal-lined bin, a pile of coke. From time to time, for reasons which had no apparent connection with the temperature, for the coach was always oven hot, the trainman lifted the stove lid and threw in a shovel-full of fuel, whereupon billows of acrid fumes escaped to the stained ceiling and spread over the passengers. This, blended with the stench of damp clothing, the unmistakable musk of manure, plus fogs of tobacco smoke, gave substantial texture to the atmosphere.

Conversation in the coach was reminiscent of my pal the station agent at Melfort. There were never more than a dozen passengers at one time, always working men and farmers, most of them wearing dungarees and rubber boots. They tended to make terse pronouncements addressed to no one in particular, but to which someone would eventually reply with equal brevity, though with profound and absolute agreement.

"I ain't seen it this bad since '48," ruminated one weather-beaten oldster without removing his gaze from the passing watery landscape.

"Yeps," all around.

"They say over back of Tisdale the barns is just about floatin'," came an eventual reply. You could feel the general assent, not to mention sympathy for the folk back of Tisdale.

I silently studied this communication pattern for some time, impressed with the casual air of community that prevailed no matter who came aboard or left. Indeed, not wishing to be thought unfriendly, I rehearsed a comment of my own and waited for the proper opportunity to join in the conversation. When a long lull came I went over my comment inwardly once more and, trying my best to emulate what seemed to be accepted practice, kept looking casually out the window as I blurted out, a little too loudly and with a higher pitch of voice than I had intended, "I suppose all this rain will make it hard to get the seed in."

It was as though the train had come to a sudden, screeching stop. To my horror everyone in the coach turned and stared directly at me, each one maintaining his gaze for what seemed to be an inordinately long time, scrutinizing the source of the intervention which, for reasons which eluded me at the time, marked me as an outsider. Silence swallowed the clickety-clack of the wheels on the rails. I began to understand the meaning of eternity. With exaggerated interest I concentrated on counting passing telephone poles. Finally, an overalled passenger seated across the aisle spoke up.

"Ben off to college—eh?" he said, sympathetically.

"Yep." I replied, taking no risks. And that was the end of conversation for a while.

Every few miles, at tiny stations and railway crossings the train came to a convulsive stop for an exchange of milk cans, mail bags, machine parts, occasional passengers, and great volumes of information and opinion, mainly about the weather. Then the steam locomotive threw out bellows of smoke, jerking the assemblage into motion again, and more fields floated past.

As dusk approached the trainman added a new dimension to the pungency of the atmosphere by lighting the gas lanterns that hung from the smoke-stained ceiling. The lanterns hissed. Clickety-clack, clickety-clack, clickety-clack chattered the wheels, breaking off fractions of miles. Cough, cough, cough, hacked the passengers. Tears of rain angled swiftly across the outside of the window against which I pressed my face in a futile search for relief from the heat and fumes.

At last the train's speed diminished and a few low buildings slid past. Outside my window, in the grey, wet evening, a lone horse and rider galloped alongside and reared to a halt as the train hissed to an exhausted stop. It was the end of the line.

I donned my purple jacket with the gold Waterloo College letters across the back and with red-rimmed eyes, a chronic cough, and the knowledge that there had been a lot of rain that spring, I stepped into a different world.

CHAPTER 3

Carrot River

The arrival of the thrice-weekly train was something of a social event in Carrot River. Whistling, clanging, and leaking jets of steam as it approached its final destination, the locomotive rang out a warning for everyone to keep clear of the tracks. At the same time, it was a signal for those who had business, or nothing better to do, to mosey on over to the station. By the time the train groaned and squealed over the last yards of track an impressive conglomeration of folk was there to greet it.

The tradition had been firmly established a couple of decades earlier. At that time the mixed train, running once a week on tracks completed as far as Carrot River in 1931, nearly always brought at least one new family and its belongings to settle in the area. Now, a few people turned up to meet a returning family member while others were on the platform wistfully wishing they had someone to greet, or somewhere to go. Some came to pick up a parcel or a crucial part for a tractor, ordered days or weeks before. A lot of folk were there simply to see what was going on.

Among the citizens braced against the weather on the open platform that bleak April evening was the Reverend Gordon L. Toombs. It was easy to pick him out. Like everyone else, he was clad in rain gear and knee-length rubber boots, but he lacked the weather-beaten look of the other men standing about. Besides, I could see a telltale wedge of clerical collar at his throat.

He in turn had no difficulty identifying me. He took one look at the college-jacketed, oxford-shod, young man stepping down from the passenger coach at the end of the train, and began to laugh.

"You must be the student minister," he chuckled as he came forward, introducing himself with a warm handshake. "Welcome to Carrot River." There was no menace in his mirth and I could tell right away I was going to like him.

He grabbed one of my suitcases and led me from the station, single file, along a perilous path of planks laid end to end through a sea of mud towards the manse which, he explained over his shoulder, had been built by the United Church as an outpost hospital. As we approached the stubby, frame bungalow I thought of the silent history its walls contained, the human dramas, injuries repaired, illnesses overcome, the babies born, and the lives of those for whom medical help had been futile. The small medical facility had been made possible by a bequest from two Ontario sisters. The Misses Mitchell had left instructions that the money was to be used for the establishment of a frontier hospital, but they had not stipulated a location. The Church had chosen this location "on the basis of need."

More telling about the history of the community was the record of the building's construction. When the Mitchell Memorial Hospital officially opened its doors on October 23, 1935, and everything was tallied up, it was revealed that equipment costs amounted to $1,341.27. The building and lot came to $2,295.21 plus five dollars for "extra land." Seven hundred and nineteen hours of free labour had been donated. Paid labour at twenty cents an hour came to $143.80. One hundred and fifty-four horse-team hours at twenty cents an hour had gone into the project.

I was to learn these details later. Now, upon arriving at the erstwhile hospital, Mrs. Toombs immediately made a plateful of Prem sandwiches and the first decent cup of tea I'd had in days. A sense of well-being took over my weary mind and body as we sat around the kitchen table exchanging stories and getting to know each other. I was exhausted and was looking forward to a good sleep in a stationary bed. However, before I could enjoy this luxury, a price was to be paid.

My supervising pastor and Carrot River's first resident minister was a man who, due to the combination of his natural inclinations plus the isolation of his post, was starved for conversation with someone versed in the language of theology. Unfortunately, since I was not to begin theological studies for another year my knowledge of this esoteric realm was lean. Actually, it was almost non-existent, being comprised mainly of smatterings from the works of authors like J.B.Philips and C.S. Lewis. For basic doctrine I had digested *The Main Points* by Charles Reynolds Brown, and I was ploughing through John Dow's *This is Our Faith*—all safe and solid stuff for a student minister to transport across provincial boundaries, but not very meaty for a man who was to go on to become a professor of theology and who had just survived a northern Saskatchewan winter.

My confessed weakness in the subject did not deter him. Spurred on by the reasonable assumption that a candidate for the ministry would have some interest in theology, he availed himself of the opportunity to indulge in what was obviously a frustrated passion—dialectic. Gently at first, he wove wondrous thought patterns about my ears, playing them out in the rich language of dogmatics, shaping them with subtle nuances. Then he moved in mercilessly with the Socratic method, setting up rhetorical questions like tenpins before scattering them gleefully with well-aimed arguments. He forged impregnable aphorisms and moulded beautifully balanced syllogisms, arriving at conclusions which he humbly attributed—with his arms flung open, a slight shrug of the shoulders and a conspiratorial smile—to pure and simple logic. Trying to conceal my befuddlement, I agreed heartily.

I marvelled at the man's lung capacity. With only brief pauses he continued unabated. Occasionally stabbing the air with index finger to emphasize a point, he postulated and hypothesized, reasoned, argued, premised and probed, adding authority with strategic quotes from Barth, Brunner, Tillich, Buber, and Niebuhr. I would eventually read these scholarly giants, but at this stage they were no more than awesome names to me. My supervising pastor had a wonderful time. For two hours he gave me the full benefit of his pent-up winter of reading and pondering while I gave him diminishing focus and feigned comprehension.

When at last he moved off to another room, the wild gleam lingering in his eye and a satiated smile on his countenance, my hopes for sleep were momentarily raised. However, his wife, who had been lurking in the background awaiting her turn, pounced immediately.

Mrs. Toombs was a professional nurse, and had a more practical bent than her husband.

"Have you ever delivered a baby?" she demanded.

"Nope—I mean—a baby—er—actually, no," I stammered.

"Well, it wouldn't hurt to learn a few basics," she continued. "One of these days somebody is going to come due out there, the roads will be out and they won't be able to make it into town. You'll be the only one with any formal education to speak of and they will expect you to know what to do in an emergency."

She pulled a hefty medical text from a shelf and sat down beside me at the kitchen table insisting that I become familiar with the fundamentals of midwifery. The graphic details she supplied left me breathless, particularly when it came to listing all the things that could go wrong. By the end of the lesson I was formulating silent prayers—though I hasten to say, without visible slouching—that the roads would be open for all expectant mothers.

That night, in spite of fatigue, I slept fitfully through recurring visions of steam rising from cauldrons of boiling water and the piercing cries of herds of newborn babies.

Next morning at breakfast, my supervisor inquired what I had brought with me. Anxious to improve upon my weak performance at the previous evening's theological marathon, I began listing the various concordances and commentaries, devotional guides and doctrinal tomes I had lugged along as tools of the trade, so to speak. For one who had demonstrated such passion for doctrinal substance, he now seemed strangely disinterested and pressed his inquiry into the realm of clothing and footwear. An immediate priority was soon identified and I found myself following him along the treacherous planks again, this time towards Lockhart's general menswear store where he financed a loan enabling me to purchase my most important piece of ecclesiastical equipment that summer: a pair of rubber boots.

The excursion also gave me my first real look at the town. It was like stepping into a western movie set. Two rows of false-fronted frame buildings faced each other across a broad thoroughfare of mud, which "baked as hard as asphalt in dry weather," my supervisor assured me, but which was now an impassable quagmire of ruts and puddles. The one vehicle to be seen that morning was a huge John Deere tractor. It sat at a grotesque angle midway along the main street, sunk beyond its axle, abandoned pending drier weather.

It was clear that, apart from horseback, the only way to get around until drier weather arrived was by foot. The previous year some of the board sidewalks had been replaced with cement, but the roads were all still pure mud. The paths of planks had been thrown down to make it possible to get from one side of the street to the other or from one portion of the sporadic sidewalk to the next.

Travel along these narrow lanes of lumber was hazardous. Some of the boards had more or less disappeared into the muck from the weight of human traffic. Others waited till they were stepped upon to sink, allowing a thick soup of mud and cold water to envelop the ankles of the pedestrian. An acrobat's sense of balance was required to remain on the planks that could be seen, for they were wet and slippery, and frequently tilted at a dangerous angle. It was not uncommon to see someone abandon all attempts at dignity and make a wild, ungainly dash, with arms flopping like a panicking turkey, in an attempt to maintain sufficient balance to reach the next island of solid ground. The greatest challenge came when two people going in opposite directions met midway. Such encounters often tested the famed traditions of western neighbourliness.

Flat, muddy Carrot River, 172 miles northeast of Saskatoon by rail, was named for the river beyond whose northern banks it squatted. It had been established as a hamlet in 1931 by six families and one bachelor. There were stories that isolated settlers had squatted in the wet, heavily wooded area as early as 1911. But it was in 1931, when the Canadian National Railway completed a line to the tiny cluster of wooden shacks with the express purpose of opening up the territory, that a mixture of pioneers started coming north in significant numbers. They came in search of new hope, fleeing the disastrous droughts and hard times in the southern parts of the province, but also from farms, towns, and cities across Canada. By 1948 Carrot River had grown from a hamlet, to a village, to a town. By the spring of 1955, when I first set eyes on it, the population had risen to approximately 875 souls.

Small though it was, Carrot River had been a significant

lumber centre for a number of years. I had always envisioned Saskatchewan as treeless prairies of golden grain stretching as far as the eye could see—the bread-basket of the world. True enough, but I soon discovered that the geography was more varied than I had imagined.

In the south and southwest the soils and climate permitted very few trees to grow, the exception being the Cypress Hills plateau which forms an island of mixed wood. Tenacious poplar, willow, chokecherry, and saskatoon bushes cling to the soil in sheltered coulees while willow, birch, Manitoba maple, and aspen follow streams and grow on intermittent, low bluffs. In a belt known as the aspen grove running northwestward across the province through Saskatoon to Lloydminster, the same varieties tend to be sturdier where they have been permitted to stand. Beyond the great plains and the aspen grove, however, and below the muskeg and mineral-rich outcroppings of the Pre-Cambrian Shield, lie vast coniferous forests of white and black spruce, balsam, jack pine, and tamarack, part of the broad swath of forest stretching across the continent from the Atlantic to the Pacific. The town of Carrot River lay on the cutting edge of advancing agriculture as it ate into these virgin forests.

At the height of the lumbering era the northeastern belt of settlement from the Porcupine Mountains which straddle the border with Manitoba, and extending north to Meadow Lake, was busy with no fewer than 500 sawmills, many of them portable in order to follow the receding line of timber. By 1940 there were sixty mills in the Carrot River district, turning out lumber for railway ties, ammunition boxes, poles, pilings, and building materials, and supplying settlers with their main source of cash income. But by 1955 lumbering, while still active, had given away to agriculture, and the focus in the flat little town had shifted to servicing the surrounding rural area.

When I arrived in 1955 Carrot River was still a frontier

town with a tangible sense of exposure to the capricious whims of nature, and with Saturday nights that were filled with the wild whoops of late-night revellers roaring around in mud-splattered trucks. Temperamental electricity and telephone services had been installed but natural gas, sewer, and a water system were still a long way in the future. At the edge of town stood the inevitable grain elevators like giant sentinels frowning over the cluster of low frame buildings at their feet and stoically withstanding the onslaughts of northern prairie weather. The Canadian National Railway tracks and a gravel road entered town at the south side. To the north a deeply rutted dirt trail left behind what meagre amenities there were and ventured out into the wild territory of pioneer farming and scattered homesteads.

Gordon Toombs informed me that Battle Heights, where I was headed, lay six miles north along this trail, then nine miles east. A further ten miles east was Smoky Burn, the second point in my three-point charge. West of Smoky Burn and six miles south, tucked in a cleared pocket in the bush, lay Papikwan, the third point. I also learned that for nearly two weeks the mud roads had been impassable. No one from "out there" had been able to get into town and since there were no phones beyond the town limits people were uneasy about the lack of communication.

I spent nearly a week at the Carrot River manse before a truck made it into town from Battle Heights to pick up desperately needed supplies. News was abroad that the student minister had arrived and was waiting for a ride. Hitching and offering rides was a way of life to these people, so before leaving town the driver came by the manse and offered to take me with him, though not before having thoroughly quenched his thirst at the Empress Hotel. The ensuing journey turned out to be one of the most harrowing experiences of my young life.

It was late afternoon by the time we churned through the

partially dried streets and headed out of town. The one-ton
Fargo truck had oversized wheels and heavy-duty everything,
and belonged to Barney Thiessen, the storekeeper at Battle
Heights. As I was to learn later, Barney was a more refined
man, a non-drinker, with a less extravagant vocabulary than
the present driver, whose name was Bob. Bob had a crinkled,
crimson face with a lot of loose skin around the neck and two
or three yellow, tusk-like teeth which must have collected
plenty of dust on dry days. Slouching at an angle in the
driver's corner of the cab, he held the steering wheel at the
twelve o'clock position with his left hand while trying to roll
cigarette makings with the other. He spilled a lot of tobacco,
and showed what I considered to be a very casual interest in
the whereabouts of the road, such as it was, all the time
keeping up a running commentary on the stupidity of
Ottawa, the treachery of Liberals, and a few other subjects of
special interest to him but which I failed to note due to my
preoccupation with our impending doom.

We hit the first mud hole at about forty miles an hour. The
truck leapt like a sumo wrestler attempting to do the broad
jump, not quite making it off the ground. With a sickening
thud it landed nose first in the centre of a thick soup of gumbo
and water. For several terror stricken miles I had been rigidly
braced against an imaginary foot brake on my side of the cab,
with one hand on the dash. Consequently, the force with
which my head struck the windshield was mercifully reduced.

I glanced at Bob. He was still slouched in much the same
position, driving with one hand. But a change had come over
his countenance. Now his face was lit with an undeniable
glint of grim glee. In that moment I saw him as he really was.
He was not driving a truck at all. He was riding a bronco.

As we plunged into the mud Bob slammed his foot against
the accelerator. The truck jumped forward like a spurred
stallion. It bucked, sideslipped towards the ditch, lurched

forward again, shuddered, and began to founder. Just then Bob let out a blood-curdling whoop that rose above the roar of the engine and the whine of the straining transmission.

"Yahoooo! Come-on ya sonofabitch—git outa here," he urged. The response was immediate. The truck dug deep in search of traction, the wheels kicking up gobs of mud that battered the fenders and shot out behind in a black rooster tail. Then, with what seemed to be a last frantic effort, it bounded forward, climbed onto firmer ground and shot ahead towards the next mud hole.

I took stock of my bruises. Bob, on the other hand, resumed his tirade against Liberals and easterners as though the episode had been nothing more than the interruption caused by one of the frequent relightings of his crumpled cigarette.

Even when we were not churning through mud holes the trip was hair-raising enough. The roads of this outlying region had been built in the thirties by teams of horses pulling earth-moving scoops and by gangs of men with shovels working ten-hour days for thirty cents an hour. Two parallel ditches were dug and the road was formed by throwing the dirt from either side up between, relying mainly upon the passage of traffic to compact it. The resulting surface could be as hard as iron given sufficient sunshine and a fair load of traffic to pack it down. However, a few minutes of rain converted it into slippery gumbo that clung to wheels and boots like glue and made driving treacherous. When this happened travel was impossible. Everyone stayed home, or wherever they happened to be, until the roads dried.

The first person to attempt passage invariably did so too soon following the rain, perhaps because he was, "wherever he happened to be," rather than at home, or for some other reason of urgency or embarrassment. The soft dirt would be cut with deep ruts by the wheels of the first vehicle, ruts that bore visible testimony to the traveller's whereabouts and his careening journey, but which also established an almost unavoidable set of tracks for subsequent traffic. Eventually, as a result of differing wheelbases and oncoming vehicles passing at various points along the route, and in no small measure, due to the individual idiosyncrasies of western drivers, these dirt roads became corrugated with intertwining ruts and ridges which grew firm as the gumbo dried.

Bob's method of driving was to get the wheels into the major troughs and to give the truck more or less free rein. The trouble was that he drove about three times faster than the tracks had been laid. The jarring, lurching, and jolting did not seem to bother him. Only when we jumped out of the ruts and headed for the ditch would he condescend to apply corrective action, and then it was mainly verbal.

Including stops to inspect bad mud holes while rubbing one's chin, it took a terrible two hours to cover the fifteen miles to Barney Thiessen's general store. When we finally got there the truck was covered with mud and I was bruised but strangely exhilarated. I had, "made my way," as my letter of instruction had directed, to Battle Heights.

CHAPTER 4

Battle Heights

Barney Thiessen's general store was half of the business district of Battle Heights, the other half being Stan Wilson's garage and gas pump across the way. Both places were strategically situated at a T-junction where the dirt road coming from the south butted into the one from Nipawin going east towards Smoky Burn. Indeed, Thiessen's place stared directly down the north-south "correction line," or "the market road," as it was sometimes known, because it had been built in 1934 by hand and horse power so that settlers could haul grain to market at Carrot River, after the railway reached that far.

Although Barney and his family owned and ran the store, large black lettering across the false front of the clapboard building declared that it was "Bill's Store." This apparent discrepancy caused no concern among the locals however, because they all had fond recollections of the previous owners, Bill and Vi Boschman, who were now somewhere in New Zealand. Barney had seen no reason to change the gradually fading sign which was a nostalgic reminder of the corner's history.

The store's origins went back to the earliest days of settlement in the area. A fellow by the name of Tom Andrews came north from Aylsham in a covered, horse-drawn cutter back in the winter of 1932. With rough lumber from Ryan's sawmill—one of several in the district—he built a fourteen by eighteen foot general store on the ridge west of the T-junction, on a clearing belonging to Andrew Rowan, Battle Heights' earliest settler. Within three years Tom Andrews' store burned to the ground. So, he built again on the same spot, larger this time. The new building was an ambitious twenty-two by twenty-four feet.

Bill Boschman bought the place in 1939, and under his proprietorship the store gave a measure of focus to the widely scattered district known as Battle Heights. Bill, like many of the settlers in the region, had moved north to get away from droughts and hard times in the southern parts of the province. He spent some time in and around Carrot River when it was no more than a cluster of shacks. Then, in January of the year, shortly after marrying his landlady's sister, he and his new bride pushed further out into the frontier. With a sleigh piled with groceries, ammunition, axe handles, and a ton of flour, he stocked the shelves and went into business.

That same spring, before the snow melted, the building was jacked up, set on sleighs and pulled by eight horses from the ridge to the location at the T-junction. George Horne, the overseer of the project, did such an expert job that none of the stock was removed from the shelves and Bill stayed open for business throughout the whole exercise. The only damage was one broken oil-lamp chimney that toppled from a shelf.

Axe handles and ammunition were well-chosen items with which to stock the frontier outlet. Every acre of land had to be cleared by back-breaking toil in those early days. Trees, from eighty to over a hundred feet tall and from ten inches to two feet in diameter, were felled by axe and crosscut saw. They were used to build the first log houses or were sawn into rough lumber at one of the many mills. Stumps were pulled by horse power and piled into windrows to be burned. Meanwhile, the forest, which was being nibbled away by the bite of the axe, was replete with wild game, which was hunted as the principal source of meat. The axe and the .303 rifle were companion instruments of survival. They were natural stock for a frontier store.

Not that Bill had much hope of being paid in cash for most of his wares. Money was the scarcest commodity in the territory. Squirrel hides, which were fetching as much as eleven cents each around the time the store opened, could be traded for some nails. Eggs and butter were bartered for flour. Horse hair or lumber might be turned over for credit. It was the only way business could be carried on and Bill and Vi understood this. They felt they were building something for the future, and their confidence was demonstrated by the fact that Bill, who was interested in horticulture, experimented with planting varieties of fruit and ornamental trees as well as a magnificent vegetable and flower garden, creating a park-like oasis in the harsh wilderness of mud and flies.

This early venture into merchandising at Battle Heights had been perfectly timed to fail. In September of the year Bill bought the place, Canada entered the war against Nazi Germany, and by the following year the whole territory was drained of much of its population as people left to join the forces or to work in urban factories. Bill also joined, and the store, which had become a symbol of community for the scattered pioneers, was shut down for several years. Land clearing came to a standstill and wherever cleared areas were not cultivated the forest crept back with young poplar and birch. Many of the original settlers who survived the war found easier ways of earning a living and never returned to Battle Heights. When "Bills Store" reopened in 1946 the population of the area was only one-third of the pre-war level.

All of this I learned later from Barney Thiessen who, with renewed but almost equally ill-timed ambition, had bought the store in 1951, just in time to suffer the consequences of "the wet years." Barney was a wiry, swift-moving man whose face and frame had been shaped by hard work and exposure to weather. He really didn't look much like a storekeeper, for his early upbringing on a dried-out farm east of Saskatoon, where he and Bill Boschman had known each other as boys, was deeply etched into his features. During the war he had been an air bomber navigator in the RCAF. In common with so many northern pioneers, he possessed a practical versatility that enabled him to turn his hand to scaling lumber, trading furs, hauling firewood, or wrestling forty-five gallon drums of gas for delivery to remote farmsteads. Hidden behind this practical, hardworking exterior, however, were remarkable talents and attributes which I was soon to discover, and which would have a profound effect upon my stay in this remote outpost.

Barney had not squandered any paint on the structure since he took over. But then, neither had Stan on his establishment across the way, and since they were not in competition anyway—except that they both sold gas—there was no need to indulge in wasteful show. Still, as the Fargo skidded into the muddy yard on that cold, saturated evening, dreary with heavy clouds hanging close to the earth, the frontier shop stood out incongruously, a dab of fading white in a muddy, winter-worn land, a small symbol of human fortitude and enterprise at a place where civilization met wilderness.

A few mud-splattered pickup trucks were parked in the broad yard as Bob backed the Fargo to the front door. When we entered the dim interior of the store, the trucks' owners were gathered about the wood stove, a bunch of rubber-booted men who turned in unison to assess this year's model of the student minister.

It was one of the remarkable mysteries of this frontier community that, with no telephones, electricity, or passable roads, news still travelled at the speed of light. Although I didn't realize it at the time, these men had taken to the treacherous roads, not only to pick up mail and supplies, but out of curiosity, possibly at the behest of their wives, because rumour had it that the student minister was arriving, and they all wanted to find out what sort of young, green, whipper-snapper the Church had sent them this time around.

Of course, I was anxious to make a good first impression. It seemed to me that since leaving Ontario all my attempts at verbal communication had been less than satisfactory. I didn't feel that I could cope with another volley of "yeps" and "nopes." So, after some unceremonious introductions, before the ensuing silence got out of hand, I turned to the only available alternative, which was to help unload the truck.

With energy designed to impress, I hurled myself at the task. Urging Bob to stack yet another layer onto each successive load, I staggered into the store on buckling legs, depositing my burden before sprinting back to the truck for more. Cartons of canned goods and tinned milk, cases of pop and bags of flour, bales of dry goods and barrels of nails—I lugged them all in a frenzy of activity that saw me lapping the slower-paced slug-gards in rubber boots. Sweat broke out on my brow. Off came the college jacket. Up came the shirt sleeves. Then, back at it faster than ever. More boxes. More bags.

The first inkling of fatigue arrived, fairly soon actually, with the emergence of a recurring vision I could not seem to shake. It was a picture of a cold glass of water. The image grew more and more compelling and rapidly assumed the propor-tions of an obsession. I was dying of thirst. Why was it so hot? And why were there so many items still on the truck? I began to flag, just a little. Yet, I had to make a good impression, so I forced the pace.

Now, I too was wearing rubber boots. Unfortunately, I had not yet grown accustomed to them, and that's the reason, I'm sure, that I suddenly tripped while heading into the store with a particularly tall load of boxes, the contents of which were unknown to me. With stark terror at the realization of where I was headed, I went pitching across the floor towards the wood stove, balancing before me the leaning tower of boxes. While I was fairly certain they did not contain crystal china, I nevertheless felt they should not be allowed to fall. The consequent contortions, I was told later, reminded one fellow of a young moose in a hurry on a frozen slough.

I believe my cargo and I would indeed have gone crashing into the stove had big Charlie Parker not stuck out a mighty tree trunk of an arm to stop me. No one actually said anything at the time. Nor was there any change in the pace of the unloading, apart from my own temporary incapacity while regaining composure and executing an elaborate investigation into the structural deficiencies of the sole of the offending rubber boot. I'm not sure, but I thought I detected traces of bemused smiles on the faces of the other men.

I did notice that none of them was sweating or gasping for breath. None of them had stopped to take off a jacket or to roll up his sleeves. This little bit of work didn't warrant such measures.

I muttered something about how there must have been mud on the sole of my boot. Charlie Parker wondered aloud where on earth such a substance might have come from. Nevertheless, the explanation appeared to be generally accepted and I resumed my duties, though at a less ardent pace, fitting into the steady rhythm set by the others. In no time, it seemed, the truck was empty.

Once the job was finished there was still a fair bit of standing about to be done, for the place had always been more than a retail outlet. True enough, the little shop stocked and dispensed an amazing range of goods and services, from slabs of bacon to lag bolts, combination underwear to crochet hooks, chicken wire to patent medicines, including a toothache oil that certain characters bought in large quantities for the purpose of soothing deeper aches of the soul. Barney had a strong sense of social responsibility. He tried to control sales of this potion, but it was difficult to determine the extent to which weekend epidemics of toothache were genuine. Vanilla extract was always kept under the counter, for there were fellows who could not be trusted to bake with it.

From six in the morning till eleven at night the Thiessens dispensed medicine, handled mail, and provided items of necessity and modest pleasure to their far-flung customers. However, the most important function of the little store and post office was social. Most evenings, when the two gas lanterns were pumped up and lit and were hung to hiss from their ceiling hooks, a handful of settlers could be found standing about the stove, nursing a bottle of pop in a work-swollen hand, or sipping a cup of Ann's coffee while lambasting politicians, or working up a petition about the roads, or discussing with intimate sympathy the difficulty someone's cow had calving, or worrying about the incessant rains. The store was a community centre for the exchange of vital information, for airing opinion, and for testing common sense. It was a place for frontier farm people to meet and visit with their neighbours. By helping unload the truck I had earned a place about the stove that April evening, and thus began a relationship with some remarkable people.

One of these persons was Charlie Parker who, with the out-thrust tree trunk, had saved me from calamity. He was a ruddy-faced, barrel-chested man who moved without haste but with a relentless air of purpose. After an appropriate period devoted to chat and banter Charlie explained that I would be staying at his place and suggested we should be getting on our way. A bit dismayed at the thought of another bronco-busting ride, I nevertheless gathered my bags and hat and followed Charlie to his truck.

We turned left from the store, passed Stan's garage, and headed east in the direction of Smoky Burn. The Parker homestead was just a mile along the road. Although the brooding evening was well advanced, daylight lingered in the northern sky and on either side of the road I could see the cold, wet fields zippered with windrows. In the gloom of the dying day, bluffs of trees left standing around low swales, or as windbreaks for lonely homesteads, stood silhouetted like eerie galleons on a motionless ocean. Heavy brush-cutters and breaking ploughs drawn by Caterpillar tractors had replaced the broad axe and horse teams of earlier days, but land clearing was still far from complete. The dense forest stood to the north and surrounded the clearings.

The land was flat and I couldn't understand why the place was called Battle Heights. Charlie explained that the "height" of land was the slight ridge just west of the store. This ridge had been formed by the receding waters of the prehistoric, glacial Lake Agassiz. Local lore had it that in the shale and sand of this beach line, arrowheads and other archaeological evidence of a fierce battle had been found, giving the place its name. "Well, at least, that's what they say," said Charlie, as we lumbered over the mud.

Out here the road was less mature and, if anything, was even more slippery than the miles from Carrot River. But Charlie was a saner man than Bob behind a wheel. His body and character were built in perfect proportions to the land he inhabited: large, strong, and alert, with an economy of word and movement that gave a sense of strength to everything he said and did. His massive frame made the truck seem small and manageable beneath him as he deftly eased it around pot-holes and washouts.

Not that there were no jolts or bumps. There were plenty. Indeed, Charlie had just pointed out the one-room school-house where I would be holding church services when we dropped into a bad rut and the truck was thrown about violently before it could be steered out. Between us on the seat were my two suitcases. On top of them sat my hat. I had been steadying the cases with one hand but the latest lurch threw the hat to the muddy floor of the cab. I reached down to fetch it and began brushing it off, a touch self-consciously.

I looked at Charlie. He seemed to have moved his gaze away off to the end of the road, concentrating on where we were going in grand terms rather than fussing with the details of what lay immediately ahead. His broad-brimmed hat had an unapologetic band and a big dirty feather sticking out of it. This was a hat that could shelter a man from the sun and the rain and its ample brim would flop with some distinction in a wind. It was stained with the sweat of many summers and it sat comfortably on his noble head. It was a hat to be admired.

I glanced down at mine. How puny and lacking in masculinity my clean, city-slicker specimen seemed to be by comparison. I felt strangely uncomfortable, consumed with a sense of inadequacy. Obviously, I would never be able to wear a hat like this out here. This was big country; it called for big hats. Inwardly I cringed at the ridiculousness of carrying a thing like this all the way from southwestern Ontario to northern Saskatchewan, and as I stared down, turning it about in my hands, it appeared to be shrinking.

Something had to be said. An explanation had to be given. Why on earth would anyone carry such an impotent headpiece into this fertile territory? I would blame it on my mother. Yes, that was it. I would never have brought it if it had not been for her. But, before I could say anything Charlie, as though reading my mind as well as the road, broke the engine-filled silence.

"Ya know," he drawled, and his sky-blue eyes still seemed fixed somewhere out there where the road disappeared into the evening. "It's a pretty good idea for a student minister to wear a hat out in these parts."

Echoes of my father's philosophy about the usefulness of hats reverberated in my mind. Perhaps my mother was not so far wrong after all. Charlie swung the wheel and brought the truck easily around a soft spot in the road.

"Yep," he continued. "A fellow should never be without his hat." It was weird, I mused inwardly, how these older guys—my father, a businessman in London and Charlie, a farmer away out here in northern Saskatchewan—shared so much reverence for hats. There had to be something to it.

We turned off the road and lumbered up a muddy driveway, lurching to a stop in the expansive yard behind the Parker farmhouse. I thought the subject of hats had been exhausted. But, upon coming to rest, Charlie grew thoughtful.

"Yeaa-ppp," he continued, drawing the sound out for emphasis. "I'd say wearin a hat would be a smart move." He paused, then as he opened the door to climb out of the truck he added, "There's a lotta woodpeckers in the bush around here."

CHAPTER 5

Life on the Farm

The Parker home was a little larger than many of the other houses in the district. It was also relatively well appointed, bearing in mind the primitive conditions throughout the territory. A huge cooking range, perpetual consumer of split hardwood, dominated the kitchen where most of the family activity occurred, its heat being a comfort in winter, a curse in summer. Water was still hauled from the outside well, and the drinking pail and dipper covered with a piece of gauze sat at the end of the kitchen counter. Charlie had rigged up a kitchen sink, which served for everything from shaving to dishwashing, and although there were no taps, it drained directly to the outside, which was a great improvement over carrying slops out by hand. With justified pride, Charlie showed me this detail as part of my orientation to the household. He also showed me the other toilet facilities. They were a discreet distance along a path behind the garden, past the icehouse. In many respects the Parkers shared common standards with their neighbours. On the other hand, a number of improvements set them a little ahead of the average in comfort and convenience.

For example, the Parker place was one of the only farms to boast electricity, of sorts. A metal, frame tower stood in the yard behind the house and when there was a breeze—something there was usually no shortage of—a two-bladed propeller whipped into motion, turning a small generator. The pulse was transmitted to a row of huge, acid-filled batteries lined along the wall in the cellar, and power was drawn from this reservoir as needed. The current fluctuated and appliances could not be operated from it, but it was electricity, and so long as there was wind enough to keep the batteries charged the evenings around the kitchen table would be illuminated with a bulb rather than a noisy, smelly lantern.

Perhaps it was this element of modernity that qualified the Parker household for the dubious honour of lodging the student minister. Or, maybe it was the fact that they had a small bedroom available upstairs, complete with a curtain across the doorway, thus providing a modicum of privacy from the two giggling teenage daughters across the narrow hall. Charlie frequently proclaimed that they got the student minister because Mary was by far the best cook in the territory. After I was with them for a while my own view was that I had the good fortune to be with the Parkers simply because Charlie and Mary were kind, generous people who opened their home and their hearts to a young fellow who was a long way from home.

Charlie Parker knew a lot more than I did about being away from home at an early age. He had been born in Iowa, U.S.A., and had lived with his grandmother till he was four. He spent the next few years with his father and stepmother in Winnipeg, but at age eleven he left home and joined a bachelor uncle near Codette, south of Nipawin, earning his keep by cutting cordwood and hauling it to Carrot River for a dollar a cord—delivered. In 1931 he settled on the homestead in Battle Heights and worked with his uncle Roy all that winter, building a log shack and barn, digging a well, and clearing brush around the buildings. That was the beginning of over two decades of dauntless hard work—interrupted by a stint in the tank corps during the war—which had gone into wresting this homestead from the muskeg and the forest. Charlie Parker was justly proud of what he had accomplished. But he had not done it alone, and he knew it. One day, when we were working together in the barn, he told me that the smartest move of his life had been when he married Mary.

Mary Parker, whose body was shaped for and by her life of hard work, epitomized the female pioneer virtues and skills which, along with the physical labour and ingenuity of the men folk, were equally responsible for subduing the frontier and establishing community life. Besides her legendary output as cook—Charlie's girth giving credence to the claims he broadcast on her behalf—this self-effacing, shy woman, quietly managed the household, tended the vegetable garden, and cultivated a showplace of flowers. She fed the chickens and collected the eggs. She made, mended, washed, and ironed clothes without the benefit of electric appliances. She "put down" pickles and bottled berries, vegetables, jams, and meats to be laid away for winter. The glossy shine on the living room linoleum was a matter of pride with her as was the texture of her homemade bread and the artistic arrangements of gladioli or dahlias she brought to adorn the schoolhouse for Sunday church service. When there was community tragedy or celebration the men put on clean shirts and showed up, but the women baked and served and looked after things, and Mary was always there. On top of all this, she found time to give birth to five children, nurturing and chiding them each into responsible persons.

For a woman like Mary Parker, taking in the student minister and telling him to set out his dirty socks and underwear for the Monday morning wash, may not have been quite as normal as baking bread and plucking chickens, but it was close. It was a natural extension of her life of caring and tending. There was community prestige to be gathered for the effort, to be sure, but Mary was neither overly impressed nor under respectful. She did some surrogate mothering but she expected me to be the student minister, and as time went on we quite unconsciously worked out an interesting arrangement.

My duties took me to all corners of the far-flung parish, but Mary's homemade pie and hot coffee were mighty incentives to return home in the afternoon, well before supper. I made a point of succumbing to the temptation on a number of occasions. Mary would carry on with her chores in the kitchen, while I fed my face at the table. Sometimes she would wipe her hands on her apron, pour herself some coffee and join me for a short break. Sometimes I shucked peas for her while we chatted. For me it was ecstasy to dig into a chunk of pie lathered with thick cream and to bask in the motherly friendship of this fine woman. For Mary it was a chance to allow conversation to amble into areas of thought and feeling not easily visited when almost every minute of every day was taken up with work. Often we talked about practical concerns such as the condition of the roads and the incessant rains, filling the brief pocket of time with companionable chit-chat that respected invisible boundaries and protected areas of vulnerability. There were other times when we ventured into more deeply personal realms, about hope and anxiety, about faith, doubt, and wonder. Mary was not demonstrably religious, but one afternoon, during one of these chats, she asked me to say a prayer for her and her family, and I did. Then she asked if I wanted another piece of rhubarb pie, and I did.

The Parker family was superbly functional. It had to be in order to survive against the forces of a harsh, isolated environment. Hard work was the dominant theme of their daily lives. One son, Wayne, was "working away" while I was with them. Cora, the eldest daughter, was married and living in Carrot River. When the roads were good on Sunday, she and her husband, Everett, brought the first grandchild, little Mary Lynne, out to the homestead to be doted upon. After church, Sunday dinner was a festival of sturdy food and family solidarity, full of wit and wisdom, in which I was always made to feel at home. Sheila was in her mid-teens and Carole was budding into hers. They were pretty shy around me until we got to know each other better, which was just before I was ready to leave. They were also industrious apprentices of their mother's wide-ranging crafts and had plenty of chores to do. Big Jim, powerful as a bear, and about as surly if he had been out with the boys the previous night, worked the farm with his father.

For a while I felt that Jim was unfriendly, for he often strode through the house with barely a grunt of greeting if I was about. He wasn't a guy to talk a lot. One wet day when the weather wasn't fit for farming, Jim was building a closet in the main bedroom, and I offered to help, pleased to be able to employ a skill in which I knew I was competent. Jim was a farmer, not a carpenter. He had just sawn a stud and was trying to put it into place but found, to his dismay, that he had cut it a fraction short. As he explained—showing that he had inherited some of his father's wry sense of humour—it was short only at one end. I replied that this was true enough but unfortunately it was the wrong end. That got a smile. I asked him if he had a cigarette package, which he produced. I folded over a couple of thicknesses of the cardboard and shimmed it between the top of the stud and the overhead plate, making it fit snugly before toenailing it into place. It was an old carpentry trick but it did more than make the stud fit. Jim and I got along pretty well after that.

Actually, I got along fine with all the people in the family. It was my relationship with the family cow that tended to be on the tense side. At least, it started out that way. Come to think of it, the chickens weren't all that fond of me either. The deterioration of my relationship with them could be traced to a mechanical source.

For transportation I had been provided with a noisy, loose jointed, limp-fendered, 1929 Model A Ford. It was a mechanical marvel that was held together by pieces of wire and electrical tape. It ran on a combination of gas, supplied at

Stan's garage, and ill-founded faith, supplied by myself. One of its more unfortunate idiosyncrasies was that it had no brakes. This presented only minor inconvenience when the roads were soft, because under these conditions the gumbo acted as a natural brake the second I took my foot off the accelerator. When the dirt was dry and packed hard, however, it was easy to misjudge the coasting potential of the thing. For example, if I happened to drive into the yard a bit too fast, which seemed to happen quite often, I was immediately faced with the choice of crashing into the icehouse, ploughing through Mary's garden, or circling the yard a few times till the vehicle slowed down. Short of carrying an anchor to throw out—an item that was in short supply in farm country— circling was the preferred choice for safe stopping.

The chickens took a dim view of this. They regarded the yard as their domain, wandering at will, clucking low-key barnyard gossip to one another. Feigning refinement with their gingerly, slow-motion steps, but betraying their true nature by pecking off flies and scratching the earth in search of treats, they asserted territorial title, not only by the haughty bearing they assumed, but also by laying down a generous carpet of droppings that discouraged unnecessary visitation by other creatures. The spectacle of a noisy, metal monster suddenly charging into their midst and chasing them in circles was a noticeable intrusion into this otherwise idyllic existence.

Just the same, I felt that the riot of panic and protest they set up on such occasions was excessive, and it certainly drew more attention to my arrival than I desired. They staged total pandemonium, complete with hysterical squawking, attempted take-offs in every direction, crash landings, and feathers flying all over the yard. Even long after the old Ford was quite stationary they would break into renewed cackles of complaint as two or three of them recalled with shudders the horrors they had just been through and how they had never seen the likes of it.

They carried it too far. It even got that an audible wave of unrest would pass through the flock whenever I appeared in the yard, with or without the Model A. One big rooster actually rose up to his full height on a couple of occasions, craned his neck and hurled abuse in my direction while beating his wings on his chest, challenging me to stand up and fight like a man. We ate him one Sunday.

The petulance of the poultry didn't bother me nearly as much as my difficulty in establishing a positive bond with the cow, for I really liked her. It was, for the most part, an unrequited affection. The milch-cow held an important place in the make-up of any pioneer farm family. The separator and the butter churn standing in the back porch were indispensable pieces of equipment through which her twice-daily contributions were processed, constituting a cornerstone of the family diet—the blueish, skim by-product going to the pigs if there wasn't a calf to feed. Naturally, the family cow was treated with considerable respect, one might even say, solicitude.

The Parker cow was no exception. She was a Guernsey, demure, and with a somewhat regal air about her. Her self-contained aura, coupled with her place in the order of things, made me hesitant about offering to milk her. However, I wanted to prove myself useful in a practical way, so after observing the procedure a few times and feeling that a fellow with two-thirds of a B.A. ought to be able to master the art quickly, I broached the subject with Charlie. With surprisingly little hesitation he agreed to show me the basics. The cow was not consulted, however, and in retrospect, this may have been a crucial oversight.

On the appointed day I approached the front end of Her Ladyship, as opposed to what Charlie quipped was "the udder end," and spoke gently to her, attempting to establish a relationship. She was chewing on a mouthful of hay just yanked from the crib and appeared to be quite indifferent. Charlie was standing close by, ready with instructions. I plunked the stool down and took up my position.

"You'll hafta get a bit closer," said Charlie, as I attempted to reach the milk-producing appendages from a distance of about eight feet. Reluctantly, I scraped the stool closer by increments, each minute advance being urged upon me by Charlie till he had my cheek right up against the warm, distended belly of the beast.

"It might be a good idea if you had the pail under there," he suggested. I must have been a touch apprehensive, to have forgotten this elementary step. Reaching back, I retrieved the pail from the eight-foot mark and placed it strategically where I soon expected to have a steady stream of milk flowing. Next I prepared my hands. I figured it might be quite a shock for a cow to have something cold placed on such a tender area of the body, so I blew into my cupped hands, rubbed them swiftly together to get the circulation going, wiped them on my pants, clapped them together a few times, flexed my fingers, then looked underneath. I hesitated. A problem I had not contemplated confronted me. Fortunately, Charlie was still close by where I could consult him as to which of the protuberances were on tap.

Charlie handed me a cloth with instructions to wipe the udder and teats before starting. I dusted off the whole assemblage the best I could, anxious to avoid anything that might have been mistaken for fondling. Then I went to work. The cow suddenly stopped chewing. Laboriously she turned to look over her shoulder at the source of annoyance by her side. Two big, brown eyes fixed me with weary gaze. It was an expression of long-suffering and forbearance that was on her gentle face, and she kept me transfixed till the message of what she saw worked its way through her sluggish brain. I spoke to her in soothing tones, promising to be gentle and repeating, "Nice girl. Nice girl. That's a nice girl." At this she heaved a belaboured sigh and withdrew her gaze. Then, she promptly arched her back and relieved herself, copiously.

The barn was too small to accommodate the full extent of my hasty retreat. Stool and pail in hand, I was somewhere out in chicken territory before Charlie caught up and began persuading me that there was nothing personal in what had happened and that I should try again. It was a longshot, but I asked the question anyway and was not surprised at the reply.

"No," said Charlie, "There'll be no issuing of gas masks." He did have one suggestion, however. "Might be better," he drawled, "if you used more than just one finger 'n thumb." With a faint grin he added something about the need to "fully grasp" the situation if I was to be successful. I wasn't sure I would be able to abide his puns all summer.

Since I couldn't conjure up a pastoral emergency requiring my immediate attention in Smoky Burn or Papikwan there was nothing for it but to return to the barn where, as a now necessary preliminary step, Charlie delivered a short course in the use of shovel and broom and how to sprinkle fresh straw.

It was while engrossed in the complexities of this task that I had a powerful revelation about the relevance of my academic training. For an instant it all became clear. Political science, sociology, philosophy, psychology, the history of the world, and what I was shovelling—the whole works—in an instant of blinding truth, I realized, were one in substance. Sad to say, insight that comes suddenly is prone to dissipate with equal speed. The spell was soon lost and I have never again been quite as clear about the relevance of much of what I learned in college.

It would be wrong to say that the rest of the milking went without incident. Yet, somehow I persevered, and so did the cow. At one point she did swing her weighty head around to look at me again. There was a lot of white showing in her eyes and I was afraid we were in for a repeat performance, but she contented herself by delivering a resounding slap to the side of my head with a wet tail. Eventually, Charlie took over and finished the job with a commanding rhythm that sent streams of milk swooshing into the pail on top of my hard won squirts and dribbles. I was never more relieved to see a job finished. Charlie said he was sure glad I had helped him, for it had only taken three or four times as long as usual. The whining barn cats were ecstatically happy to see the task completed, barely allowing time to have their dishes filled before plunging their faces into the warm milk. However, no one was more relieved when the ordeal was over than the cow herself, and for a long time after this she eyed me with grave suspicion whenever we met. I felt it was a pity we hadn't hit if off. She had a nice face.

Developing rapport with the various animals on the Parker farm was an ongoing challenge, to which I applied myself with less devotion than St. Francis of Assisi. Speaking to birds, as he is reputed to have done, was one thing. Attempting to chat with a bunch of hysterical chickens, however, seemed to lie beyond the ascetic tradition, particularly since I sometimes assisted in their slaughter for Sunday dinner. The horse was friendly enough, but tended to be the strong silent type. With the pigs, I couldn't get a word in edgeways and soon gave up visiting them. But, for some reason I was drawn to the cow. I never again attempted to milk her, but from time to time I went to see her and she seemed to grow accustomed to my presence. There was something beautifully mystical about staring into her big, brown eyes in the dim and musky atmosphere of the barn. Slices of light cut angular patterns through the dusty air and it was quiet, save for the muted music of her munching, or the trombone of a bluebottle caught in the tangle of spider webs around the window. The barn was a sanctuary. I even grew to relish the rich incense of hay and manure and would go there when I had a few minutes to enjoy the sense of peace, and in some strange way, to silently commune with the cow.

And are you sometimes lonely, cow,
standing long and ruminating?
Or, do you ever think,
while whipping pesky flies?

If achieving an appropriate degree of intimacy between man and beast presented a challenge, in the realm of human interaction a different kind of difficulty emerged. It had to do with preserving a comfortable measure of personal privacy. That this should be a matter of concern at all became clear on my first Saturday evening on the Parker farm.

Saturday was the day I prepared my sermon, so I was at the diminutive desk in my room most of the day. Late in the afternoon I slipped downstairs to help Mary clean up some one-hour-old pie she didn't want to go bad. Jim had come back from the fields and after downing a piece of pie himself, he set about building a fire in the yard under a gigantic, black cauldron suspended by chains from a tripod. Meanwhile, the girls rushed back and forth filling the great pot with buckets of water from the well. I had no idea what was happening until Mary casually mentioned that it was bath night. Always anxious to prove myself useful, I offered to help with the preparations, but I was told that they had a system and that everything was under control. I decided to get back to the sermon which, on account of the pie, seemed best contemplated, at least for a while, from a horizontal position. As I lay back on the pillows I began thinking about how bath night was going to be accomplished.

I knew there was no bathroom, and the idea of getting into the cauldron in the middle of the yard invited uncomfortable images of perished missionaries on other frontiers. Not that I suspected anything intentional. But, what if a fellow were bathing and somehow the fire got out of control? One could easily boil. I could just imagine the furtive blinking of the chickens maintaining an uncharacteristic conspiracy of silence as they watched me turn to stew. I could feel the rising heat and then, through the waves of steam, I saw them gathering in a chuckling circle around the cauldron. Gaining confidence as they realized that I was doomed, and urged on by the crowing of the shaman rooster, they began pecking at my last vestige of urban propriety as it floated on the frothy surface of the soup: my hat. I was boiling and I seemed powerless to help myself. I could even smell my own flesh cooking, a rich, yeasty smell, it was. The mounting heat sapped my will. I knew that if I didn't act soon it would be too late. Summoning every last ounce of strength, and in defiance of the mocking hens, with one ultimate, determined effort I leapt frantically from the pot and landed with a thud on the bedroom floor.

"Are you all right," yelled Mary from the kitchen, where she had just taken a pan of loaves from the oven and from whence, through the ventilating grill in the floor, the sweet smell of fresh bread and the heat from the stove wafted into my room. I replied the only way I could think of at the time.

"Yep."

They did have a system for bath night, and considering that every pailful of water had to be carried into the house and lugged out again after use, the procedure made a lot of sense. Off the end of the living room was a storage room in which the flour bin, a bag of rice, un-ironed laundry, the broom, and sundry other items were kept. Here a zinc tub, which usually stood on its end against the wall, was placed in the middle of the floor where it was filled with enough pails of hot water from the cauldron for the first bather. I cannot recall the exact dimensions of the tub but I remember marvelling that Charlie could get into it, or having got in, could ever extricate himself from it again. The order for bathing, as best I could figure out, was based on the area of skin to be washed. Carole, the youngest and smallest, was first, then Sheila, using the same water plus an added hot pail-full if necessary, followed by Mary, for whom another hot bucket-full was drawn from the cauldron. When the women folk were finished the two girls hauled the used water, pail by pail, and poured it among the flowers and vegetables in the garden. Then the process was repeated by the men, Jim going first, followed by Charlie. I, being the student minister, was afforded a clean bath all to myself in spite of my feeble protests. Carole and Sheila, at their mother's behest, had my tub all ready by the time it was my turn. The only concession they would make to my expressed desire not to be treated differently was that I could haul out my own used water.

The trouble I encountered was that the house was not completely square or level, and the door of the storage room had a tendency to swing open. I have no idea how the other members of the family contended with this. Perhaps they all knew some secret method of wedging the door shut. Besides, I believe the men made themselves scarce when the women were bathing and vice versa. By the time I made my way towards the tub, everyone seemed to be milling about the living room, enlivened by the effects of their baths and by the fact that it was Saturday evening. If the family wasn't going into Carrot River, it was about the only time the living room was ever used. No one had warned me about the door and I had just folded myself up and lowered my body into the narrow receptacle when, perhaps as a result of someone walking across the living room floor, the door clicked and swung wide open. There, in full view, was the whole family engaged in various pursuits: Jim rolling cigarettes, Mary taking up her crochet, Charlie paging through *Reader's*

Digest, and the two teenage girls preparing to play *Snakes and Ladders*.

The door was beyond reach, at least out of hand's reach. Swiftly, I shot out a leg to push it closed. The effort, while an admirable feat of agility, was too much for the lightweight tub. It tottered precariously and for a horrible moment I feared I was going to tip out onto the floor with full contents. I managed to steady the vessel by quickly shifting my weight, like canoeing, only with the water inside instead of around the craft.

Immediate disaster had been averted. Nevertheless, a considerable wave of bath water had sloshed over the edge and was now advancing across the linoleum towards the bag of rice. It was a perplexing situation: on the one hand, not wishing to remove my foot from the door because of modesty, while on the other hand, fearful that I would flood the family rice supply, which lay at the opposite end of the room from the door. I desperately looked around for a solution. The broom! Unfortunately it was far away, standing against the wall in a corner. The chair, draped with my clean clothes and towel, was just within reach. I dragged it into position, scattered the clothes and towel onto the wet floor in the process, and with my free foot pushed the chair the remainder of the distance till it came up against the door. This manoeuvre required assuming a fairly undignified posture. With both legs fully extended, and with the exertion required to keep the door closed with one foot while moving the chair with the other, I had slipped farther and farther into the tub. Getting out without tipping was a challenge that took me to the limits of my gymnastic ability. I spilled another pailful of water in the process, but managed to extract myself eventually. Using the towel that was supposed to dry me, I mopped up the tide just before it reached the sack of rice. If anyone wondered why it took me so long to have my bath, or why my clean clothes were sopping wet when I emerged with pails of water for the garden, they were discreet enough not to ask. On future bath nights I made sure the chair was tightly against the door before immersion.

There was one other area of human activity that resulted in a certain degree of consternation on at least one occasion. It centred around one of the great institutions of frontier life, an indispensable element in any homestead, a tradition that contributed profoundly to the character and fortitude of the western pioneer, and a common denominator undergirding the widespread sense of humility in which these hardy souls took pride. There it was, architecturally humble, sometimes looking a bit forlorn off by itself, but nevertheless proving its imperturbable worth by withstanding the onslaught of winter gales and the blistering heat of summer sun. It was known by many names, this worthy institution, but since I was the student minister, the only term allowed to fall intentionally upon my tender ears was "the outhouse."

True to his nature, Charlie had built his facility just a little grander than the average. A two-holer, it was. Painted white inside and out, and with hardly any cobwebs, it boasted a bench equipped with the luxury of a couple of store-bought, splinter-free seats. In the corner sat a pail of lime with an empty can for scooping an appropriate application. From a nail at the right height, studiously perforated near its binding, hung a copy of Eaton's catalogue which, among other uses, could be read.

There was a wooden latch on the inside and normally one could rest assured of privacy in this place of comfort. However, on warm days there were persuasive arguments for leaving the door open, the view over Mary's flower garden being something of an inspiration. If anyone happened to start down the path that approached from the left, an occupied signal could be sent out by whistling a little tune, or coughing loudly or singing, or if the party kept coming, by yelling "I'm in here." Usually, there was no problem with this arrangement.

One sunny Sunday after dinner, before heading off to conduct the afternoon church service at Papikwan, I was the occupant when I heard footsteps coming along the path. I whistled the first bars of the opening hymn, which should have been enough to stop any potential intruder in his or her tracks. But the footsteps kept coming, and I thought I detected a sense of urgency in the pace. I broke into song. Still the steps advanced. Paroxysms of coughing had no effect either, and before I could actually make my presence known with words, Charlie appeared in the doorway. There was a desperate look in his eyes.

"I'll hafta join you," was all he said. I had never seen Charlie in such a hurry and, indeed, had no idea he could move so fast. With a swift flick of his suspenders and one graceful motion he was instantly beside me on the unoccupied seat. I immediately took up a consuming interest in the fabrics being offered by Eaton's the previous winter.

With no where else to go for a while, Charlie and I had a good chat that day. Later, upon reflection, I concluded that nothing in any of the courses I had taken or would ever take, no amount of pastoral psychology nor human relations training, would ever do as much to bring minister and parishioner together, as a two-holer outhouse.

CHAPTER 6

Getting Around

For the student minister on the Battle Heights, Smoky Burn, and Papikwan pastoral charge, simply getting around was a major preoccupation. The ten miles of road from Battle Heights, running east to Smoky Burn, passed through a stretch of thick forest and across the capricious Carrot River before opening out again into cultivated areas. Nearly four miles east of the iron bridge a primitive road headed south six miles to Papikwan. It passed over a low-lying bog that in the future would support an impressive peat-moss industry but which, when I was there, frequently failed to support me and my vehicle.

At each of the three locations stood a one-room school-house where church services and vacation Bible schools were held. The farms, however, were scattered, some of them completely isolated, and since visitation was considered a major ministerial function, some means of transportation was needed.

The two-door, Model A Ford, Tudor Sedan supplied for this purpose, besides being an inveterate chicken chaser, had other unique features that added colour to the history of the Church's home missions and which subjected me to challenges for which my training left me ill prepared. The car had belonged to Francis Trembly, a Battle Heights "old-timer" who let it be known by word of mouth that it was for sale for fifty dollars. A meeting of parishioners was held and Stan Wilson was authorized to buy it as transportation for the student minister. He went to see Francis to strike a deal, but when he explained what the car was wanted for, Francis gave it to the Church, even though he was Roman Catholic. "It's for a good cause," was all he said.

This was no ordinary car. Pressure of competition had caused Henry Ford Sr. to bring the Model A into production in 1927 as a reluctant concession to market demand for greater comfort and finer appearance than had been available in its legendary predecessor, the Model T. By 1929 the Model A surpassed all other American automobiles in sales. Now, here was one of that vintage ploughing through the mud of northern Saskatchewan, gallantly finishing out its days in the service of the Church. Henry Sr., with his Irish Protestant background, would have been proud.

Although something of its original lustre had been lost in the brushed-on, dark-green coat of paint it wore, and though the leaky roof was cracked and crusted with many applications of tar, I knew the vehicle at my disposal had been a thing of considerable pride and serviceability in its day. Sadly, that day was now over a quarter of a century in the past. Yet, in spite of its dilapidated appearance, the Model A retained that defiant air that is the hallmark of good breeding. Cracked fenders and all, it could still kick up an impressive cloud of dust when the roads were dry, or hurl heroically through seas of mud where more modern vehicles quickly became mired.

The windows were "automatic." With any amount of vibration they automatically slipped down about halfway, thus allowing swarms of flies and bloodthirsty mosquitos unhindered access to whomever was inside. Likewise, when it rained, in the brief interim when travel was still possible before the road's surface deteriorated, water pelted in upon the driver, and any hapless passengers foolhardy enough to have accepted a ride.

Once in the passenger's seat there was little hope of escape until released, for there was no handle on the inside of the door. Indeed, the outside handle worked only sporadically, causing awkward delays from time to time. The problem on the driver's side was almost the opposite. Here the door latch spring had long ago lost its resolve. Pieces of bailing wire laced through the windows and wrapped around the door post kept the door from swinging open at inopportune moments. This worked well most of the time. On one occasion, however, before I got used to the system, it caused considerable embarrassment.

I had been in the community just a few days and decided to drive over to Barney Thiessen's store one evening to drink a bottle of orange Crush and see who was there. The roads were navigable but it was still impossible to get equipment onto the land, so I figured there would be a few folk standing about the stove, talking. It would be a good way to get acquainted. I drove into the yard in front of the store and, by carefully gearing down, managed one of my better endeavours at stopping somewhere close to where I wanted to go, in this case, right at the front door. A couple of pickup trucks were already in the yard and another swung in beside me as I turned off the ignition. The occupants of the truck, a man and woman whom I had not yet met, climbed out and headed towards the door of the general store.

I had it in mind to alight from the Model A with aplomb and to greet the couple cheerily. Unfortunately, I momentarily forgot about the wire and automatically grabbed the door handle in an attempt to get out. Nothing happened. A rattling of the handle and a little shove only had the effect of tightening the twists on the wire, which I now noticed, somewhat sheepishly. The couple from the pickup were about to enter the store, but had hesitated, and were now staring curiously through my windshield. I smiled and waved, pretending to be in no hurry to get out, whereupon they nodded and went into the store. I tried to undo the wire, but since I had broken off the ends to keep them from scratching my neck while driving, I found it impossible to unwind the stub of twisted wire with bare fingers. I pushed on the door. I threw my weight against the door. I lunged at it. I crashed against it.

A single strand of wire would have snapped. One strand, had it been loose enough, could have been bent back and forth and broken by fatiguing the metal, as I had done to get rid of the loose ends. However, I had taken the precaution of wrapping quite a few strands of the stuff around the door post. Thus reinforced, the wire would not give, and my efforts had only succeeded in further tightening the twists.

By now, squadrons of mosquitos were flying in, fuelling up around my ears, and taking off through the half-open window on the other side. I had to get out of the car. Ecclesiastical poise was no longer a priority. The opposite door, being handleless on the inside, held no prospects of escape. I could see only one alternative. Rolling the window down fully, I eased myself over the sill, head and shoulders first, balancing my hands on the running board and then in the mud, as body, legs, and feet followed.

When I entered the store, everyone in the dusky interior was far too posed. Rigid with nonchalance they were, as though holding their collective breath for the taking of an old calotype portrait. I knew they had all dashed frantically to take up their positions, having watched my antics through the store's front window. I nodded hello and pulled an orange Crush from the cooler. The lid clinked noisily into the stilted silence as I eased it off on the opener and moseyed over to place an elbow on the counter before taking a long swig in as western a style as I could muster. A rivulet of brown stain ran up my wrist, the by-product of cooler water and mud.

"Nice evening," I threw out, economically. It was, in fact, a lousy evening, dull, forbidding, and chilly.

"Yep," came the chorus of agreement. Silence followed. I

had never known orange Crush to be so noisy going down. Eventually, I believe it was Dean Sauder who spoke up.

"That's some lock ya got on the door 'a that there preacher car," he said. I was in the middle of another swig of Crush.

"Yeppppsss," I spluttered, while orange pop fizzed up my nose and ran off my chin. Suddenly, the tension was broken and the whole place burst into laughter.

I hung around for an hour or more, chatting, listening, learning. Throughout the history of the territory, it appeared, there had been a plague of vehicles with bad door latches, a deficiency that had caused "no end of trouble" for the various owners.

When it was time to leave I slid my seven cents across the counter for the bottle of pop, and Barney produced a pair of pliers. "You might be needin the loan'a these," he said, with a wink. Barney was a real swell guy.

The Model A had other eccentricities. For example, one of the headlamps dangled from its mounting like a loose eye on a mutilated teddy bear. When driving after dark this jittering light danced and nodded from road to tree top, from ditch to horizon, one second scanning the ruts in front of the wheels, the next, soaring off to join the ballet of the northern lights. It must have been unnerving to the occasional oncoming driver on those lonely lanes of mud. Perhaps the dangling eye explains why they were always cowed over to the edge of the narrow road as I whizzed past—a rattling phantom in the night.

My relationship with the Model A was affectionate. There were times, however, when the requirement for patience was enormous. One of the less endearing behavioural oddities of the vehicle was its balkiness at starting. Indeed, starting the engine was a fairly elaborate exercise. First, the hand throttle lever had to be opened two or three notches, and the spark retard/advance lever on the steering column had to be set at the fully retarded position. Next, the carburetor dash adjustment was turned one full turn to the left. Then, after making sure that a rock—used in lieu of the non-existent parking brake—was placed in front of one of the wheels, the choke was pulled out and the ignition turned on. There was a pitted starter button on the dash, but it didn't work, so starting involved the use of a crank that was inserted and properly engaged through a hole below the radiator.

The crank could be lethal; using it called for strength, timing, and adroitness. One deft turn would sometimes induce the engine to wheeze into a coughing, spluttering spasm of life, that had to be followed up immediately by a dash to push in the choke, advance the spark, and adjust the throttle while pumping the accelerator. Usually this ritual needed to be re-enacted several times. Even though I sprinted from crank to driver's seat at speeds that would surely have broken the four-minute mile, which was the record to be broken in those days, I generally arrived at the levers and accelerator just as the engine shuddered and died. When the engine did take hold and the door was securely wired, the gear stick was shifted into low, the clutch was let out, and gas was applied, often enough no forward movement ensued. At this point, it was a good idea to get out and remove the rock.

Of course, a turn of the hand starter might just as soon result in a convulsive backfire and a "kick" from the crank that could break an arm or send a church-dressed student preacher sprawling in the mud. I discovered all of this to my sorrow early in my relationship with the old Ford, and while I was always swift enough to avoid serious injury, the vehicle's obstinacy, especially on Sundays when I was heading out to hold church services, often left me in a mood quite out of keeping with the spirit of peace and good will appropriate for the conduct of divine worship.

As time went on I got pretty good at flipping off the distributor cap and adjusting the points, or wrapping the cracked wires leading to the spark plugs with electrical tape, or draining the sludge from the improved Zenith carburetor bowl, or kicking the wheels.

This latter recourse often proved to be the most effective intervention and might have been even more rewarding had I not been constrained by awareness of my position in the community. The student minister could not be discovered assailing a poor, dumb machine with a tirade of profanities, even though, as I found in my travels around the farms, this appeared to be a fairly universal method of getting various pieces of equipment to work. Unable to avail myself openly of this approach, it is not surprising that there were many occasions when my meagre mechanical talents, even when aided by a little surreptitious cuss and a touch of physical abuse, failed to persuade the thing to go. Being towed by tractor to Stan's garage became an embarrassing part of my image in the community.

The task of keeping the student minister mobile fell naturally to Stan. He and Nelly supported the Church's efforts in the community. Stan's contribution was to service the Model A and to "fillerup" with British American Oil Company gas. The hand-levered pump pushed the amber fuel up into a glass reservoir marked off in gallons, and it was drained by gravity into the car's ten-gallon tank, the last half gallon or so being coaxed from the hose by lifting it up above the level of the gas-tank intake situated right in front of the windshield.

It was difficult to understand why Stan and Nelly had left a landscaping business in Burnaby, B.C., to build a garage and blacksmith shop across from "Bill's Store" at this muddy fringe of civilization. I learned later that Stan's real ambition was to farm. The garage was an interim measure, but in the meantime, being the only professional mechanic in the district, he was always frantically busy, especially at planting and harvest time when a broken implement could be disastrous to a farmer.

Stan was usually, though sometimes marginally, good natured about fixing the Model A, for this imposed unprofitable demands upon his time. I believe his most ardent supplications on the Sundays he came to church were that he would not see the Model A again till the student minister went back to college. On a few occasions, having hitched a ride from wherever the old Ford had decided to quit, I could pick out the occasional familiar word from his muttering as he saw me approach with my tale of woe, and I strongly suspected that he may already have been addressing himself to the Almighty, in no uncertain terms.

Quite apart from the unpredictable nature of the Model A or the condition of the roads, the most formidable barrier to travel east of Battle Heights each spring was the Carrot River. Named for the wild carrot plant found growing along its banks, the river's outflow begins in a series of lakes, marshes, and capillary-like creeks, southwest of the town named after it. The Carrot is already 100 miles long by the time it reaches Smoky Burn and it has drained an area of 3,290 square miles of flat farmland, carving a deep, meandering channel into the plain that was once the bed of an ancient glacial lake. Gathering volume from tributaries that weep down from the heavily forested Pasquia hills to the south, it follows the imperceptible tilt of the land towards the northeast, flowing roughly parallel to the mighty Saskatchewan River further north, but eventually joining it near The Pas in Manitoba.

Normal spring run-off had always swelled the river into an impressive surge. In the heyday of logging this served a useful human purpose. Thousands of logs would be stacked on the ice awaiting spring break-up, at which time they would be flushed downstream to the mouth, there to be boomed and towed by stern-wheelers down the Saskatchewan to the mill at The Pas.

Lying within the great boreal forest region, the whole Carrot River watershed, prior to the arrival of European settlers, had been covered with luxuriant stands of spruce, poplar, balsam, and tamarack. Jack pine and birch stood on drier ridges that were the beach lines of the receding prehistoric lake. In low, marshy areas, layers of moss and peat from one to three feet thick acted like gigantic sponges by retaining moisture and releasing it gradually. As the forests receded before the plough, the character of the spring run-off changed. Snow that once melted slowly in the shade of the timber now converted swiftly to running water under the full glare of the sun and the fanning of spring winds. Severe flooding was the inevitable result.

Then came the wet years. Starting as early as 1948 and lasting through till 1957, Nature dumped unprecedented amounts of rain on Saskatchewan. Average annual precipitation in the Carrot River area had normally hung around fifteen to sixteen inches. The early fifties saw annual rainfalls of thirty-six to thirty-eight inches in some parts. The river could not cope with the run-off. Every spring it became a raging torrent, clawing at its banks, ripping out trees, washing away bridges, and flooding the surrounding land.

Successive bridges on the road between Battle Heights and Smoky Burn had been swept away by the spring floods. The river could come up overnight, perhaps in a matter of hours, and even in the years when the bridge survived, the half-mile-wide valley became completely inundated, and the communities were cut off from the outside world, sometimes for weeks at a time.

I had been in Battle Heights for a couple of weeks and was growing restless to explore the territory and to meet the people on the other side of the river. Besides, I was supposed to hold church services in each of the three points, and I was eager to carry out my duties. The river was in flood, however, and the road along the valley floor was under water. Until the day Alf Sauder arrived in the Parker yard, it looked like it might be a long time before I would see Smoky Burn or Papikwan.

Alf Sauder's homestead was the next one west of the Parkers. On the day he wheeled into the yard, no cars or trucks had been moving on the roads. Alf was driving his tractor, and was pulling a flat wagon with metal-shod wheels and a long, single shaft. Sitting on the cart amid a mess of mail bags was a rubber-booted fellow with his hands shoved into the pockets of a muddy parka, a rifle hanging on the crook of his arm, and a slouching, tweed cap hanging on his head. It was Bud Kowalsky from Smoky Burn.

At first glance Bud cut a menacing figure, sitting up there in grimy clothing carrying a bare rifle. A friendly smile soon spread over his face as he climbed off the wagon with Alf jumping down from the tractor behind him. Bud and his wife, Louella, ran the shack-sized co-op store and post office at Smoky Burn that year. He was taking a load of mail into Carrot River, but how he got this far was a mystery to me, for I knew the road west of the bridge was still under several feet of water. No wheel-driven vehicle could possibly have crossed. When I found out how he and Alf had linked up to ensure that the mail got through, an idea began forming in my missionary mind.

Alfred, Howard, and Dean Sauder were well-known brothers who had been around Battle Heights since 1934. They characterized the hard work and individual ingenuity that was necessary for survival in this demanding frontier. They also exemplified the community spirit and neighbourliness that made life tolerable. That's why Alf was driving the tractor with Bud sitting in the wagon.

By now the communities on the other side had been cut off for several weeks. No mail went in or out during that time and supplies at the co-op store were either exhausted or running low. Something had to be done. I never learned who owned it, and it didn't seem to matter, but a boat of sorts had been built so that in emergency, once the worst rages of flooding had passed, it was possible to get across the river. Bud was driven by tractor from Smoky Burn to the river. Meanwhile, Alf drove to the river from Battle Heights with his tractor and wagon. When Bud crossed the river and the flooded flats using the boat, Alf was there to meet him and take him into Carrot River with the bags of mail and a pocketful of shopping lists. How they had managed to arrange timing was another one of those mysteries of frontier communication, for there were no phones.

Bud had taken the trouble to look for me at the Parkers. He wanted to let me know that quite a few of the people in Smoky Burn were looking forward to having church services. Together we worked out a plan and Bud assured me that when he got back to the other side he would pass the word that church was to be held in the schoolhouse the following Sunday.

The congregations had agreed that the morning service would be held in the community where the student minister was lodged that particular year. A three o'clock service was scheduled for Papikwan, but as yet I had not spoken with any of the people from that district. An early evening service was to be held in Smoky Burn.

On the Sunday following my meeting with Bud and Alf, I conducted the morning service at Battle Heights. After dinner with the Parkers I pulled on my rubber boots, cranked up the Model A, and headed for the river. It had rained the night before and travel was difficult, but the Model A ploughed through and I reached the river without serious incident. Leaving the car well back I walked to the lip where the road dropped down into the flats.

The scene below was one of devastation. The whole valley was filled with muddy water. Ever moving, the river slid ominously among the willows and alders, and swirled in sinister, shifting eddies over the submerged road. It lapped at the near bank and surged with malevolent strength in the main channel. The turbid water swept with sinister force, its surface littered with debris: branches, roots, pieces of timber, logs, and gobs of mud-stained froth. Towards the far side of the valley near the main channel was the iron frame of the bridge, slightly askew and looking like a stranded barge awash in the tireless current. Bud was waiting for me in a small backwater below the spot where I stood. He was keeping the boat against the bank by holding onto the branches of a bush.

"Better hurry. She's risin," he yelled up by way of greeting. "She's a whole lot worse now than when I came across an hour ago," he added, betraying a note of worry. The run-off from last night's rain was just now making itself felt. "I figure she's come up more'n a foot in the last hour," said Bud as I scurried down the slope with a load of ecclesiastical equipment necessary for my job. We loaded the boat and I climbed in.

The word "boat" was a munificent title for the craft. Actually, it was just a few rough-sawn boards nailed together and sealed with roofing tar. Flat bottomed and stubby, the tiny vessel would have presented a challenge of balance and direction to a seasoned mariner crossing a duck pond. Navigated by frontier farmers in the swirling, debris-cluttered current of the angry river, it was nothing short of miraculous that no lives had been lost, and as Bud and I pushed off, the possibility that this might happen was uppermost in my mind.

Religion has its paraphernalia, and a heap of it now sat in the middle of the boat. It consisted of a portable, wooden lectern, a drape embossed with the United Church crest, a brass cross, and a pair of enormous, wooden collection plates. I sat up front with a rough-hewn paddle in my hand and a

sermon in my pocket. Bud occupied the stern, where a battered outboard motor was mounted.

We paddled for a while through the shallow water, picking
a course close to the bushes and trees, which we sometimes
used to maintain our position or to pull ourselves forward. We
edged further up-river in preparation for what we knew would
happen when we made our bid to cross the main channel.
Well above the bridge Bud pulled the starter and the motor
spluttered to life. We left the relative security of the bush-
broken eddies and launched into the turbulent current.

Immediately we were swept downstream at a frightening
speed. I paddled furiously to aid the moaning motor. Chunks
of debris clunked against the side of the flimsy boat and water
slopped over the edge. Bud pointed the vessel at an angle
upstream and we ferried towards the opposite bank, but we
were still being taken downstream at an alarming rate.
Something heavy bumped the boat and spun us around. Bud
struggled with the motor. I paddled. More water slopped over
the boards. Several inches of water sloshed back and forth
around our feet and the United Church paraphernalia piled in
the centre of the craft. I thought of the collection plates. They
might be useful for bailing if much more water came in.

The bridge seemed to be rushing up to meet us. Sieved
from the ceaseless tide, a mess of logs and branches were
pressed against the railings of the structure. We were doomed
if the current carried us into this thrashing, groaning entan-
glement of debris. Neither of us spoke. Bud opened the
throttle of the egg-beater motor. I paddled as hard as I could.

It seemed like an eternity, but at last the bridge slid behind
us and we bumped against the bank. We had made it without
getting wet. Holding onto a piece of rope tied to the bow, I
stepped out of the boat into what I took to be a shallow
puddle. My foot sank into the muck and a deluge of muddy
water rushed into my rubber boot. I was stranded, one foot

fixed in the gripping mud and water, the other in the boat, which now began to slide back into the current. Desperately, I grabbed the paddle. Using it as a stilt I somehow managed to pull my foot from the boat, but the only place to put it was beside its mate. The boot filled up. I looked back at Bud. He too had stepped in over his boots.

We tied the boat to a tree and sloshed up the bank with our cargo to where Bud had left his truck. "Well," he said, philosophically, as we both leaned against the fenders pouring water from our boots. "We made it without getting too wet."

That evening, a good crowd of hardy, farm folk gathered at the Smoky Burn schoolhouse. Before the service began, Rosemary Armstrong, the volunteer pianist, rendered a few numbers designed to transport frayed spirits into a mood preparatory to worship. I listened incredulously. She was playing "Shall We Gather at the River."

CHAPTER 7

Stick in the Mud

Soil surveys in the physiographic division of Saskatchewan known as the Carrot River Lowlands where Battle Heights, Smoky Burn, and Papikwan are situated, speak esoterically of hydromorphic and podzolic soils overlaying a parent formation of glacial-lacustrine sediments. What they really mean is mud.

From an agricultural point of view the soils of the district vary according to location, from bog and muskeg to sand and shale, though the best arable soils tend to fall within the association known as Tisdale heavy clay, with some Arborfield clays. Rich in nutrients and massive in texture, these soils can grow crops of grain yielding sixty bushels an acre and more. But, in the early years of settlement, before adequate drainage was established and with the wet years adding to the problem of surplus moisture, whatever the agriculturalists and agronomists called it, in the experience of the people who lived there, it was mud.

Mud made life what it was for the settlers. A wet spring meant late seeding. With a growing season averaging only about a hundred days between killing frosts—even though long hours of northern daylight compensated for the short season to some extent—late planting almost assured immature grain or frost damage by harvest time. Soggy fields in the fall rendered harvesting difficult or impossible, sometimes causing crops to be abandoned to winter.

Mud was everywhere. It splattered vehicles and stained the skirting of buildings. It kept people's feet plugged in sweaty rubber boots. It paralysed cars, trucks, and tractors in its mucilaginous grip. Farmers spent a lot of time helping each other haul equipment out of sloughs; they spent a lot of time "getting stuck" and "getting un-stuck."

Perhaps the most spectacular story of getting "un-stuck" was the time Gordon and Delia Rowan's tractor became so mired on a trail out towards the Pasquia hills, that they literally blew themselves out of the predicament. Placing a circle of partial sticks of dynamite around the tractor, which was up past its axles in sloppy silt, they blasted the mud away sufficiently to lay down a corduroy of branches upon which they were able to drive out of the quagmire. Miraculously, both they and the tractor survived. Most measures were less extreme. Yet whether it was trudging to the barn to do chores or getting an injured neighbour to Carrot River for medical attention, mud was a dominant feature of existence in those early years.

Getting stuck in mud, or being stranded by it, was also an inevitable part of the experience of the student minister, providing him with what could be loftily reported in the courts and chronicles of the Church as "the profound learning opportunities afforded our students for the ministry." I, myself, don't recall any profound learning opportunities associated with being stuck in mud. I do remember quite a lot of muddy misery and discomfort attempting to get to the schoolhouses to hold church services or trying to visit scattered farms.

Mechanical balkiness aside, the Model A could not be faulted for the times it got stuck. Indeed, when it came to getting through bad road conditions, its high-wheeled carriage and ample fenders made it superior to more modern, low-slung automobiles, and many a time I managed to travel when locals wouldn't venture onto the roads with anything less than a tractor. As a result, I developed a foolhardy sense of optimism about "getting through" which, in turn, earned me a reputation for recklessness. When I was lucky, people were amazed at my mobility. When I got stuck, they shook their heads and hauled me out.

One of the main problems of travel on the mud roads was that the particular type of mud throughout the region—commonly known as Saskatchewan gumbo—had a tendency to adhere. Actually, it was more than a tendency. It stuck to everything. Instead of simply falling off the wheels of moving vehicles, for example, it wrapped them in ever thicker accumulations, and as clumps of the stuff did eventually get thrown off by centrifugal force, it built up between the wheels and fenders till the whole assemblage became bound and immobilized. When this happened, the best way of getting the mess unclogged was to take the wheels off the vehicle.

Something like this happened one Sunday as I headed to Papikwan in one of my many futile attempts to hold a church service there. When I started out, the road east from Battle Heights had a few wet spots, but nothing to cause serious problems. However, after turning south towards Papikwan, the surface grew softer with every mile. No trace of traffic marred the road since the last rain. This gave an ominous sensation of venturing into uncharted territory. A haunting isolation gathered about me as the tires of the Model A squished deep ruts into the virgin surface and the chatter of the engine was diminished by the din of gobs of gumbo whacking against the insides of the fenders. I was driving as fast as I dared, hoping to forge ahead by sheer momentum, but the heavy traction dragged on the wheels and burdened the engine. The car lost speed. I gave it more gas. The engine strained, but to no avail. Slower and slower, laboriously, chugged the Model A, till it finally shuddered and almost stalled. I stepped on the clutch and swiftly geared down, gaining a few more feet in second gear before the car threatened to go into mechanical convulsions. I geared down to first, but in a moment the transmission protested again and as I slammed the clutch to the floor the car came to an abrupt stop in the middle of the empty road. I turned the ignition off. Save for subsiding creaks and sizzles under the hood, a vast, lonely silence descended upon the scene in which I found myself.

An inspection revealed what I already knew. The wheel wells were solid with mud. I had no tools with which to attempt picking at the packed gumbo and no jack for taking off the wheels. Anyway, even if I had, in a short distance they would have gummed-up again. I took stock of my position. To the south, the black, rain-washed road ran straight to a point on the horizon. From the north, two careening ruts snaked up to the tires of the stationary Model A. In the flat emptiness that lay in every direction there were no sounds of human existence, no voices, no barking dogs, no noises of motors. I would have to walk.

Shod in my rubber boots but dressed for church in white shirt and tie, with a city-slicker, belted, trench coat over all, I started out along the trail, pursuing the tracks cut by the Model A. I didn't get far. The properties that caused the mud to stick to the tires of the car now made it stick to my boots. In no time both feet were laden with heavy accumulations of gumbo that rolled up over the insoles of the boots and clung around my ankles in weighty wads till I could barely lift one foot after the other. Stopping every few steps to shake the worst of it free proved ineffective and exhausting. I was mired. Hip-socket rending suction and the heavy clusters of clay made progress impossible. I did the only thing I could think of. Reluctantly, I pulled off my boots and socks, rolled up my pant legs, and trudged barefooted through the cold, slimy muck, carrying a rubber boot in each hand.

It was at this juncture in my experience as a student minister that I, apparently, somehow, completely missed a "profound learning opportunity."

I must have walked a mile or more when, from a side trail up ahead, a tractor wheeled onto the road and bore down towards me. I don't remember who it was. I only know that when he stopped and invited me to hop on behind, I loved him with all my heart. We got to the Model A, hitched onto it with a chain and dragged it like a stubborn heifer back to drier road. Then, from the tool box under the seat of his tractor my rescuer pulled a large screwdriver and a tire iron, and for the next hour we probed and picked till we cleared enough space around the wheels to enable them to turn. There was no church service in Papikwan that Sunday, and when I got back to the Parker homestead, having driven barefooted, I went straight to the pump in the backyard.

After this experience I tried to be more prudent about venturing onto wet roads, assessing the situation carefully before starting out, taking fewer risks. The consequence of this newfound caution was that I got stuck again. Only this time it led to the most frightening experience in my whole pastoral apprenticeship. It happened near the bridge.

For some reason the grade forming the easterly approach to the bridge always presented special problems. Here the road had a tendency to remain wet and slippery long after most of the surfaces had firmed-up. Because it rose fairly steeply from the river to the level of the land, vehicles often had difficulty climbing the slope, or descending it without sliding over the edge.

The road seemed well packed and relatively dry as I drove towards Battle Heights late one evening after having had dinner with the Trites family of Sunnydale Co-op farm. Don and Helen Trites, like most couples in Smoky Burn, were swamped with endless hard work, raising a young family in the barren comfort of their small home. Don was a stocky man with a big voice and a friendly smile. Helen had a slightly shy air about her. They were unassuming folk who, in spite of their own daily difficulties, often reached out to their student minister with a word of support and encouragement. It had been a pleasure visiting them, and perhaps it was the ensuing sense of well-being as I sped through the gathering dusk that caused my attention to wander and my speed to increase. Momentarily forgetting the condition of the grade, and inimitably oblivious to the car's lack of brakes, I went sailing over the lip of the road where it descended towards the bridge.

I had experienced some difficulty climbing the grade earlier in the day but had managed to find sufficient solid ground to get through without mishap. Now, too late, I realized that further damage had been done to the road's surface. A tractor had obviously gotten into trouble on the slope, spinning its wheels and quarrying deep gouges out of the hill as it slithered from one side to the other. It had left behind a mess of craters and mud piles that resembled a road about as much as a cake of fresh cow manure resembles a bone china dinner plate.

The wheels of the Model A were drawn inexorably into the gullies dug by the tractor, but I don't believe they ever really reached bottom; for between the deep channels, a mountain of mud had been thrown up, and onto this, with a sickening thud, landed the Model A in a perfect bellyflop, its velocity only serving to pack mud into the undercarriage and around the bottom of the radiator. I tried rocking the vehicle by swiftly changing gears from first to reverse and back again. It was hopeless. The wheels simply spun without traction. I shut the ignition off, knowing all too well that I was thoroughly "hung-up," a state of being that I have worked hard to avoid ever since.

It was now almost dark. The chance of someone coming along this late in the evening was remote, so I started to walk. I picked my steps near the edge of the grade where the mud was not churned-up, then clumped over the hollow-sounding

planks of the bridge, conscious of the rippling river beneath—
the sinister sound of its licking at the abutments rising from
the murk. Along the flats I strode, the flop-flop of my rubber
boots being absorbed by the silent brush on either side.
Onward I marched into the growing darkness, into the deepening knowledge of my aloneness on this frontier trail of
packed mud.

I plodded up the incline on the west side of the flats, glad
to leave the oppressive valley behind. Palisades of tall spruce
and poplar now closed in against the road, making the darkness complete. The noise of my rubber boots offended the
utter stillness of the surrounding night as I doggedly trudged
forward, guided by faint light from the ribbon of sky between
the jagged tree tops.

Sometimes tripping on ruts or rough places, I plodded on
through the eerie blackness, fighting vague anxiety by rea-
soning with myself that there was absolutely nothing to fear;
and the more I reasoned, the more I longed to be in the comfort and safety of the Parker home, and the more apprehen-
sively I peered into the black abyss of the forest where, I knew,
there was indeed nothing to worry about—except, maybe a
ravenous timber wolf, or a pack of coyotes, or an enraged
mother bear, or a mad moose that might charge from the
bushes, or a cougar prowling afar from the Pasquia Hills to
the southeast.

The realization that there was so little to fear was a great
solace to me, and I dwelt upon it with every step—especially
the cougar. Thus comforted I decided that since I had about
another three miles to go, I should do a little gentle jogging,
just for variety, so as not to bother the Parkers by coming into
the house too late. I would run at least till I got out of the
menacing blackness of this forested area.

Down the middle of the road I stampeded full tilt, my
cumbersome rubber boots thrashing as fast as I could make

them go, "thrrrumpety—thrrrumping" through the blackness that surrounded me till, at last, the heavy timber gradually thinned to sparser brush standing silhouetted against pale light from the north, tossing spooky shadows across the road.

Exhausted, I stumbled forward, reduced to walking again while catching my breath. Then, I heard it. A twig snapped. The sound cracked the silence around me with the sharpness of a rifle shot. It came from the murky shadows of the brush just beyond the ditch and slightly to the rear of where I now stood, petrified in my tracks. I stayed motionless for several moments, listening. Nothing. There was nothing but the silent darkness and the lurking shadows and the sound of my own heart thumping in my chest.

Fearfully alert now, I resumed walking with gingerly step, straining to hear any sounds other than those of my own rubber boots. I went only a few steps when I heard a movement. This time there was no mistake. It was not imagination. There were footsteps on the other side of the ditch. A living creature was lurking there, obviously tracking me down. When I moved, whatever was in the darkness also moved. When I stopped, it stopped.

"Wolves Devour Student." "Cougar Attacks Cleric." "Bear Mauls Minister." The hackneyed headlines flashed in my imagination. I would have taken up jogging again but I didn't want the predator to get the impression that I was afraid. Besides, my legs were now more like rubber than my boots. I decided to walk on. The beast followed. I could hear branches being swept aside and the swish of grass and dead leaves. It was a big animal. I could sense the weight of its steps. Again I halted. It stopped too, no doubt ready to pounce. Cautiously I resumed walking while watching over my shoulder, and a moment later the relentless stalker pursued. Fumbling in my pocket I found my penknife. I opened the blade. It was an impotent two inches long. Precisely at that moment of vulnerability my worst fears were realized, for as the sparse brush finally opened onto a field of windrows, and eerie moonlight splashed over the shadowy landscape, to my horror, I saw the beast's form emerge. It was monstrous. Its head rose above the bushes skirting the ditch and stood clearly outlined against the faint glow of light from the north, fresh moonlight glinting in its wide-set eyes. From deep in its throat it uttered a low, mournful sound. "Moo."

When my heart recommenced beating, the relief was enormous. Apparently the cow, or steer, was as lonely as I was in that vast, empty night. It walked along beside me on the other side of the ditch, keeping me company for quite some time, till it must have reached a fence, for the noise of its presence ceased. My fear was spent now, and while I tramped forward, past Agnes and Henry Schüler's place on the left, and the Eriksson's half a mile further, the whole northern sky was lit in a symphony of cosmic glory as Northern Lights danced their splendiferous ballet.

I too skipped and danced, charged with unspent adrenalin and stirred by the magnificent natural display. Soon I turned left onto the Parker's road, then left again into their yard, shushing the dog as I approached the back door. It was a beautiful night. Almost too nice to go indoors.

A story circulated throughout the territory about the student minister who was visiting a remote farm one evening when it started to rain. It rained hard and soon it was obvious that there would be no travelling on the roads, so the student was invited to stay the night, and he graciously accepted. As members of the family made preparations for bed the student minister got up and went outside, everyone assuming he was availing himself of the facilities. But, as time passed and he didn't return, anxiety mounted. Eventually, it was decided that the farmer should go to the outhouse to see if everything was all right, at which point the student minister burst in through the back door, drenched and covered in mud.

"My goodness, look at you, you're drenched. What on earth happened to you?" he was asked.

"Well, you know, I had to go home for my pyjamas," he replied.

It was a tale that was told at my expense more than once, but it was a generic story that I believe may have been applied to every student minister who ever served the region. And, it was a true enough story too—up to the part about the pyjamas. I spent many a night on a chesterfield or spare cot, having been stranded by rain and mud. But, the time that was etched most fondly in my memory was the night I spent with Ann and Barney Thiessen and their family in the cramped living quarters behind the store.

Barney and Ann were Mennonites so they didn't come to the church services in the schoolhouse unless it wasn't possible to get to their own church four miles south of Carrot River. However, they were always encouraging and supportive and we became friends. The wet years brought hardship for the Thiessens as well as for the settlers, for there was little cash in the community and many of their customers had been forced off the land. To provide service and to capture every possible opportunity for business, the store was open from six in the morning till ten or eleven in the evening, six days a week. So if I wanted to visit them, it had to be by hanging around the store, or sometimes going in the Fargo with Barney to deliver a barrel of gas to an outlying farm or sawmill.

One evening I was invited to the Thiessens' for supper, after which I stayed on in the store chatting with Barney and Ann while the three middle children carried on with chores. In the shop Jimmy, an impish four-year old, amused himself with makeshift and imaginary toys, while Joy, the eldest daughter, who was brain-damaged from birth, kept reaching for my hand, asking the same questions over and over. "Where's your car? When did you get here?" At nineteen, Joy had already lived well beyond expectations; she was an example of sustenance by sheer love.

Rain had started around supper time and by nine o'clock it was clear that no one would be coming to the store that evening. It was also obvious that I wouldn't be able to leave, so the front door was locked and we repaired to the living quarters for the evening.

Barney washed his hands and took a violin case from the corner. Marian, who was about seventeen, shuffled through music at the tall-backed piano dominating the busy room. Lois, two years younger, helped Ann prepare a lunch. Dave, who was about thirteen, carried in firewood and added it to the stack beside the stove. Joy became excited as Barney tuned the violin, and I settled in for an evening of old time fiddling and country and western music, wishing I had brought my ukulele. I was completely wrong in my expectations, a victim of my own urban presuppositions.

The music began, and to my amazement, from the throat of the violin tucked under Barney's craggy features, and evoked from the sturdy body of the piano by Marian's flying fingers, there flowed beautiful baroque melodies from Bach and Handel, and the clear classical minuets and sonatas of Haydn, Mozart, and Beethoven, and romantic songs and serenades from Schubert and Schumann. I was transfixed. Here, in a narrow room behind a plain, frontier, general store, a father and daughter played a concert of amazing beauty and tenderness, while outside, cold rain lashed the harsh and rugged land.

After a while we sang. We sang "The Holy City," "The Lost Chord," and "The Twenty-third Psalm" to "Brother James's Air." We sang "I Come to the Garden Alone" and "The Old Rugged Cross," and with the aroma of Ann's good coffee in our nostrils, we sang "Bless This House." And there was warmth and joy in all our hearts. When we sang ourselves out, Barney said grace before lunch, thanking God for His bountiful goodness and mercy.

In July of 1956, during my second year as student minister, "Bill's Store" closed permanently, and the Thiessen family moved away, victims of the wet years. I missed them. Without the store, Battle Heights was never the same.

CHAPTER 8

"The Burn"

Smoky Burn came by its name honestly. In the summer of 1937 a major forest fire swept through the heavy stands of timber covering a portion of northern Saskatchewan's Pasquia Forest Reserve. Several hundred men trekked along torturous trails to set up camps and combat the wilderness blaze. When it was finally brought under control, thousands of acres of living forest had been reduced to gaunt skeletons standing against the expansive sky.

Then, in 1942, as though returning to complete an unfinished job, fire again swept the area. The first conflagration had sped quickly, killing the trees without consuming them. Now, the bleached timber acted like tinder for the advancing flames. Fire got into the thick peat moss where it smouldered for months. The acrid smell of ash was everywhere. Even after snow blanketed the earth, smoke seeped through from dangerous hot-spots deep below. All winter, slivers of blue-grey smoke hung in the still air. The area became known as "The Big Burn," or simply "The Burn." Situated over thirty miles by logging trail and fireguard from the nearest town, it was a forbidding landscape of dead timber, with fibre seared from the soil's surface, mosquito-infested swamps, and poor drainage. The surrounding forests were populated by wolves and bears.

Nevertheless, following the Second World War this apparent wasteland took on a certain attraction. Servicemen being demobilized by the thousands were converging upon cities and towns in search of employment. Others were looking for opportunities to get into farming, a futile hope for the average veteran in view of land prices.

Eager to address this situation, and to put its democratic-socialist theories into practice, the CCF government of Saskatchewan, under the leadership of Tommy Douglas, came up with an ambitious scheme to assist ex-servicemen to get into farming on a co-operative basis. In spite of dire warnings from some quarters that the region was unsuitable for agriculture, "The Big Burn" presented itself as a plausible location for the experiment, indeed, largely because the timber had been burnt off and the land would be less expensive to clear than standing forest. When the project got under way and the area was listed as an unincorporated district, it was officially named "Smoky Burn."

Quite apart from its isolation and primitive conditions, when I arrived on the scene, I sensed there was something very different about Smoky Burn. For one thing, there were no elderly folks. There were barely any teenagers, and very few single people. All of the men were veterans. Furthermore, in a way that was difficult to define, the atmosphere of the community was pervaded by the co-operative philosophy upon which it had been founded, even though it wasn't difficult to find individuals who did not subscribe to the principles. Above all, there was a palpable sense of community borne out of the common endurance of hardship.

I realized that if I was to be effective in my work, it would be important to learn as much as possible about the history of the community and its unique social structure. I asked a lot of questions and gathered fragments of information that began to fit into a comprehensive picture. Among my best sources was one of my parishioners, Frank Armstrong.

Frank was one of the many Canadian veterans looking for an opportunity to build a future following the war. He was a slight, tight-knit man with cat-like movements and a dry sense of humour. He had spent his boyhood on a prairie farm. In 1932 the family left the drought-stricken farm and headed north into the Carrot River district, working rented land in several locations for a number of years until his father was eventually able to purchase a remote and heavily wooded quarter section (160 acres) from the Hudson's Bay Company. Frank managed to complete grade eleven, which made him relatively well educated for his time and place. Following a stint in the Royal Canadian Air Force, however, it was his experience working with heavy land-clearing equipment and the practical "know-how" he had acquired while growing up on the farm, that qualified him for the job of superintendent at the land-clearing project out at "The Burn," where sixty-thousand acres were set aside for settlement.

In the summer of 1946 Frank and a crew of three men drove the first of the heavy equipment over The Pas trail then north along a fireguard. Amid the confusion of bleached and charred logs laced with wild pea, they set up the "Reconstruction Camp," the precursor of Smoky Burn. They found themselves in a wilderness of flies, mosquitos, mud, and muskeg. The most urgent task, therefore, was to establish accommodations for themselves and for those who would soon join them. There was an ironic twist to what they acquired for living quarters.

Further east along The Pas trail, beyond the place where the fireguard cut north, stood a cluster of weather-blackened shacks, each sixteen by twenty-four feet, with boxcar roofs of tattered tar paper. Forlorn and ghost-like they stood in the quiet forest, as concealed from view as the shameful history of their original purpose. Several of these abandoned and deteriorated buildings had been "freed up" so Frank and his men could haul them into place at the Reconstruction Camp. Here they would house the veterans who were engaged in the land-clearing project. The previous occupants had also been guests of the government. They were Canadian conscientious objectors who had been interned during the war and forced to cut cordwood in this remote and lonely corner of northern Saskatchewan.

Frank and his crew set up the camp, then spent the winter cutting and sawing lumber. In the spring of 1947 he was one of the resource persons at a three-day conference held in Nipawin to explain the government's plan. He also helped to select the veterans who would be eligible to work on the clearing project and who would eventually become members of the co-operative farms. Eight years later, shortly after I arrived in Smoky Burn, he explained the scheme to me.

The Saskatchewan government granted each veteran a thirty-three year lease on two quarter sections of land (a section being one square mile), with an option to purchase after ten years. The rent was set at one-seventh of the annual crop. Initially, the veterans were hired into Frank's gang to do clearing and land breaking. This work provided immediate wages, and was also supposed to enable the men to sort out who they each wanted to team up with into co-operative units. Once a minimum of 100 acres per person was broken, a group could organize and be incorporated under the Saskatchewan Co-operative Associations Act. Only veterans with a minimum of two years farm experience were eligible to participate, though a couple of years of land clearing could be credited as farm work. Although the land was allotted on an individual basis each lessee had to belong to a co-operative. A Federal-Provincial Agreement was worked out to enable each participant to put his veteran's allowance of $2,320.00 into the loan capital of a co-operative farm. The combined input of the individual members thus provided start-up capital with which to purchase machinery and seed, or to negotiate credit.

In earlier days of pioneering a homesteader was obliged to "prove-up" his land by clearing and breaking ten acres a year, which he did with broadaxe, crosscut saw, and a team of horses. The modern pioneers of Smoky Burn, with their second-hand equipment obtained from "war-assets," and working in teams around the clock, could clear and break as much as one hundred acres a day. Weather and the actual conditions of the terrain—as opposed to papers on the desks of politicians and bureaucrats—didn't always permit this level of achievement. Yet, by freeze-up in the fall of 1947, twenty-four hundred acres had been cleared and broken, enough to enable some of the veterans to organize into the first two co-ops: River Bend and Sunnydale. In the spring of 1948, between the windrows, Bill Hope and Carl Anderson of River Bend Co-operative Farm Association sowed the first bushel of registered wheat ever to be planted in this virgin soil. Seeds of grain. Grains of hope.

Meanwhile, the job of clearing and breaking land continued, even after the co-operatives were formed. It was still going on by the time I came to be their student minister. Land clearing was tedious, body bruising, and dangerous work. By times it was blistering hot or paralysingly cold. When it rained, and in boggy areas whether it rained or not, the mud could suck the mightiest machine into its grip. Two or three tractors using cables and winches would have to work together to pull the one that was stuck out of the hole. When it was dry, fine ash from the forest fires clogged the air intakes of the motors and the nostrils of the men. And always, from spring through fall, clouds of mosquitos and swarms of flies—horseflies, houseflies, deer flies, black-flies, no-see-ums, bluebottles—feasted on exposed areas of skin and crawled over food. Raisin bread was highly suspect.

At night I would sometimes watch the T.D.14 International Harvesters and Alice Chalmers H.D. 14 tractors working far across the flat land. Their lights probed the darkness like the glowing eyes of monstrous bugs. By day I witnessed trees and brush fall in an eighteen-foot swath, sliced off at the roots by the V-shaped blade of the brush-cutters. Slash, stumps, and logs were bulldozed into windrows to be burned and re-burned over time. Sometimes I helped with this job. It involved searing one's hide, but required little skill. Following the brush-cutter came the twenty-inch breaking ploughs, ripping out roots and turning over the earth, exposing it to light and air for the first time in history. I knew that this was history in the making.

I learned that by the fall of 1948 six thousand acres had been cleared and the following spring a total of six co-op farms were in operation, River Bend and Sunnydale having been joined by Sturdy, Pasquia Hills, Spruce Home, and Fairview. The married men were joined by their wives, and since they were all in the child-bearing stage of life, babies arrived at such a rate that wags were still saying Smoky Burn lay twenty-five miles from Carrot River "as the stork flies." The mud road was pushed through from Battle Heights. It was often impassable and the bridge was frequently swept away. Nevertheless, it was a shorter and a somewhat better route than The Pas trail.

There were other visible signs of community. A small co-operative store was organized, and that incontrovertible proof of existence, a post office, was instituted in the tiny community. A school was organized for the growing number of children. It operated half days in the home and under the tutelage of one of the farm wives until Lorna Miller was hired full time at an annual salary of $1,700.00. Lorna commenced classes in the new one-room school in the fall of 1949, thus bringing formal education to the school-age children and a sudden upsurge in the use of soap and Brylcreem among the few bachelors in the area. Lorna didn't last long as schoolteacher. One of these bach-elors, Carl Anderson, persuaded her that she should switch to a more promising career as his wife at River Bend farm.

Other teachers followed, and the little schoolhouse became a focal point of community life, housing not only daytime learning for the children, but Saturday night dances, community meetings, and Sunday church services conducted by a succession of student ministers. The veterans of Smoky Burn and their wives had carved a place for themselves out of the wilderness.

When I arrived as student minister in 1955, I found a community where hope was battered by hardship. River Bend and Sunnydale were still operating but three co-ops had already disbanded and Sturdy would fold before next spring. Some of the disbanded members were struggling at individual farming. Others had taken on jobs away from the area, hoping to earn enough to pay their taxes and to resume farming later. Many had simply walked away from everything. Smoky Burn was still charged with energy, resolve, and hope, but it was also littered with the debris of failed dreams, disappointments, and despair. As I was soon to discover, it was a place where a student minister would have a unique apprenticeship.

Soon after arriving in Smoky Burn I met Bill and Peggy Kowalsky. Peggy was one of several war brides from Europe and The British Isles who became part of the veterans' co-operative experiment at Smoky Burn. Her odyssey began when she and her girlfriend, Mary, noticed two Canadian Air Force fellows at a dance one Saturday evening in her native Belfast, Northern Ireland. "You can have the blond and I'll take the dark-haired one," she said to Mary. Sure enough, after a while the men came over and asked them to dance, and Peggy went with the dark-haired one. They danced till Albert White's Ballroom closed. They danced every leave Bill could get during the remainder of his eighteen months in Northern Ireland, and after he was shipped back to Canada at the end of the war, they corresponded. When a letter proposing marriage arrived from Bill, Peggy wrote back immediately saying, "Yes."

By the time I met the Kowalskys their sixteen by twenty-four foot house still sat on the twenty-inch diameter spruce logs upon which it had been built, and upon which it had been skidded from the camp to the ill-fated Pasquia Hills Co-op farm. From there it had again been skidded onto its present site on the land Bill was able to lease from the government when the co-op broke-up in the spring of 1951.

The tiny home now had a door with real hinges, and the windows had real glass. When Bill and Peggy first moved in, a rough, plank door leaned against the jambs till Bill eventually made hinges from pieces of used rubber tire. Pieces of burlap hung over gaps in the bare wall, only slightly impeding the flow of millions of mosquitos. Now the little home was snugly wrapped in dowdy, grey insul-siding. Inside, the bare boards had soaked up some applications of paint, one wall being brush-stroke white, one green, and the other mauve. At the end of the single room, a space of about eight feet was curtained off with blankets to form a sleeping area for the whole family, now numbering six. The first two children were born in 1949 in the same calendar year. The youngest child was less than a year old, and Peggy was again in an ominous state of pregnancy. At the end of the house where the entrance was, a lean-to wide enough for a wood range had been added. Here in the uncomplicated traditions of North Irish cookery, Peggy boiled, roasted, and fried the family food.

Perhaps it was because of our common roots in Northern Ireland that Peggy and I were initially drawn to one another. But it was a poignant event in the summer of 1955 that deepened our intimacy. I visited the Kowalsky home often. For one thing, Peggy's mischievous sense of romance made her quite blatant about juxtaposing the teacher and the student minister at her table. But even after Marjorie Stuckert left at the end of the school year, I continued to be a frequent guest at the Kowalsky's noisy meal times. The baby always seemed to need changing. The other children squawked for food and attention like young starlings in a nest. Peggy sawed off thick slices of homemade bread and tossed them along with admonitions to, "Shut your mouth and eat your dinner." I once had the temerity to suggest this might be difficult for the kids to do.

Wednesday evenings were often spent at the Kowalsky home making music. Bill played the Hawaiian guitar; his brother, Bud, played an acoustic, Western guitar; and I, the least accomplished musician of the group, whacked enthusiastically at my diminutive ukulele, vainly attempting to emulate the instrumental versatility of George Formby while forcing my Irish tenor voice to adapt to the twang of hackneyed gospel and country-western tunes.

At other times and in other homes, or sometimes at the schoolhouse, the music-making circle included Jean Borsa on the mandolin, Duff Watts sawing the fiddle, and Rosemary Armstrong chopping the piano. This was the beginning of what turned out to be an impressive orchestra, one that improved—especially after they got rid of me—to the point where they were in demand for dances throughout the territory.

Yet, Wednesday evenings at the Kowalsky home were unique. The small interior would grow steamy from the combination of body heat and the kettle's hot breath on the back of the wood range. There was Bill, always intense, his mangled arm injured in a sawmill accident moving magically to draw pure sweetness from the horizontal strings. Bud, his benign smile never fading, picked and strummed his familiar way through dozens of sung-weary songs. I watched Bud's fingers to anticipate the chord changes. The children fought to stay involved but gradually fell asleep from exhaustion. Pregnant Peggy and her sister-in-law, Louella, made us all a late lunch of tea and toast. We were a huddle of humanity in a small, wooden home, defying hardship with laughter, letting strains of music and a splash of lantern light escape into the vast, purple stillness of the northern night when one of us went out to pee. The evening ended with Bill saying a prayer of thanks to Almighty God, "for the abundant blessings He had so graciously bestowed upon us all."

As Peggy's pregnancy progressed, a sense of anxiety could be detected in the community. It slipped out in small ways, in conversation after church or when a few people happened to meet at the co-op store.

"I wonder when Peggy's going to head into town," someone would ask.

"I sure hope the roads dry up," another would say, wistfully.

"Have you seen her? She's enormous. She must've put on weight."

"Yeah, well, she'd be better to go on in a day or two early rather than wait around till the last minute."

"Yeah, you never know what the roads are going to be like."

I was a touch ill at ease myself, remembering all too vividly the midwifery lessons Mrs. Toombs put me through, although by now I realized that there was plenty of expertise among the women of the community. They wouldn't be calling upon me. The only risk lay in the possibility that I might happen to be at the Kowalsky home and become marooned by rain and impassable roads at just the wrong time. The thought was almost enough to keep me from visiting them.

The only person who seemed unperturbed was Peggy herself. After all, she was developing a reputation as a veteran in these matters, this being her fifth pregnancy in seven years. She waddled about the house and yard, attending to all but the heaviest of her endless chores, stoically awaiting her appointed time.

By the third week in August Peggy was overdue. There had been a lot of rain and the roads were badly churned up. A trip to Carrot River, even now, would be perilous. On the other hand, if it rained much more the roads might be completely impassable for days. I dropped over to their place to see how things were and to offer my help in getting Peggy into Carrot River as soon as possible. I was there less than an hour when she calmly announced that her labour was starting.

Bedlam ensued. Bill darted about getting the car ready, barking instructions at the kids. Peggy told him what clothes and toiletries to put into the small suitcase from under the bed. I raced off to the store to tell Louella so she could make arrangements to look after the children. When I came back, Peggy was walking gingerly to the car.

"Do you want me to follow in the Model A?" I asked.

"No, we'll be fine," said Bill, racing for the driver's side.

"Could you stay with the kids till Louella gets here?" Peggy asked through the open window.

"Sure. Don't worry," I yelled as the car careened out of the yard. Bill's renowned demonic driving, now fuelled with an injection of high-octane panic, caused clods of earth to shoot out behind as the vehicle swayed and swerved down the muddy road.

Next day, a farmer returning from Carrot River, came looking for me with a message. Could I get into town as soon as possible. The Kowalsky baby was dead.

I had never conducted a funeral. I had hardly ever been to a funeral. I had no idea if there was some protocol for the burial of a stillborn child, or, for that matter, whether or not the baby had lived for a short time after birth. It seemed an academic point in either case. My supervising pastor had left Carrot River and the new minister had not arrived. I would have to do the best I could. I grabbed the United Church Book of Common Order, gassed-up when I reached Stan's garage, and headed along the rutted roads, stopping now and then to determine the best path around a mud hole, almost getting stuck a couple of times, but eventually skidding into Carrot River.

It was a self-conscious, muddy, student minister who walked into the sterile atmosphere of the small hospital that dreary August day. When I entered the ward where Peggy lay, propped with pillows, all clean and white, she said nothing. She simply stretched out her arms towards me.

"Ah Peggy," said I, a hard lump in my throat. We hugged. I held the bereft mother till I felt her sobbing subside. She needed Kleenex. I sat beside her and held her hand while she told me how the doctor had broken the news to her. She cried again and I gave her more Kleenex. Bill came in. Stoical Bill. We shook hands, hard.

The three of us talked about the burial. Since Peggy wouldn't be there, I explained the brief funeral ceremony to her and, after a short prayer, Bill and I went off to make the arrangements. There was no funeral director in Carrot River, and even if there had been, Bill and Peggy wouldn't have been able to pay for the services. Bill went to secure a plot and to hire the gravedigger. I headed to the lumberyard and asked to speak to the foreman. On a piece of board I drew the plans for a simple, miniature casket and ordered the lumber, explaining who it was for, and offering the good name of the United Church as surety.

This posed no problem. It took a lot more persuasion to convince him that I was a bona fide carpenter and that he should allow me to use their power tools to build the casket on their premises. He eventually agreed and I went to work, scrounging tools, laying out the cuts. Before long, however, Roy Orchard showed up. Roy was one of the early settlers and a well-known carpenter about town. I think the foreman had sent for him, just in case. Roy offered to take over while I went to look after the paperwork. I left to obtain a death certificate from the doctor and register it at the clapboard town hall. The name on the documents was Margaret Kowalsky. The date of birth and of death were the same: August 25, 1955.

By the time I got back to the lumberyard Roy had almost completed the job. He was a good craftsman. The grisly little piece of cabinet work was taken to Roy's wife, Molly, who finished the inside with cotton wadding and an end of satin she had. The lid was left loose, with long copper screws ready to be driven in at the right time. Roy loaned me his screwdriver.

Meantime, I ran into Bill and we agreed when to meet at the cemetery. Heavy clouds scudded across the sky. It would rain soon. There was no time to waste. I drove to the hospital with the empty casket. A nurse directed me to a door at the end of the building and met me there. In a stark room used as a morgue, she laid the small form gently into the box. I screwed down the lid, then carried the coffin in my arms and set it on the back seat of the car. The Model A, now a hearse, lurched laboriously through the rutted streets. A pickup truck, indifferent to my cargo, passed me impatiently, its wheels throwing black muck out behind. Rain drops began to splatter the windshield.

At the grim, flat cemetery on the edge of town, I headed for a lone figure leaning on a shovel beside a mound of earth. He was a man in his sixties, I estimated, and he was gasping for breath. He confirmed that this was the site for "the little Kowalsky baby." Apologetically, he told me that he had a heart attack a while back and that he could dig no more till he caught his breath. He was "played out," he said. I looked into the grave. It wasn't nearly deep enough. I shoved my Book of Common Order into a pocket, grabbed the shovel and began digging, reaching ever deeper, throwing up the heavy clods of mud. Cold rain beat down. Rivulets of brown water trickled into the hole. Bill drove up and dashed to the grave side. He took over digging while I went to the car to fetch the casket, and when I returned, between us, Bill and I laid the box into the grave, both of us almost slipping into the hole in an effort to lower it with some dignity. Even then, we had to let it drop the last few feet. To my horror it wedged at an angle. In a flash Bill jumped into the hole, levelled the container in the bottom of the grave then reached up and I pulled him out. I began the committal service.

"Blessed are they that mourn, for they shall be comforted. Let not your heart be troubled . . . in My Father's house are many mansions. . . ." At the first words the gravedigger whipped off his cap and bowed his head. Rain lacquered a few strands of hair to his pale pate.

"Suffer the little children to come unto Me, saith the Lord. . . ." Across the grave stood Bill, a stricken expression on his face, his lean body braced against the bitter rain, his soul braced against grief.

"The Lord is my shepherd; I shall not want. . . ." Drops of rain crinkled the written words and wind whipped the pages of the service book. Water was gushing into the grave now. The coffin was beginning to float.

"For as much as it has pleased Almighty God to take onto Himself the soul of this child, Margaret, we now commit her body to the ground; earth to earth . . ." Thud! The gravedigger solemnly threw what he intended to be a sprinkling of earth into the grave. It came off the shovel in a sodden lump. ". . . ashes to ashes. . . ." Splash! Another clod of mud. "Dust to dust . . ." Thump!

Three drenched men stood beside the grave of a baby girl who would never climb onto her daddy's knee. Three wet, shivering men, doing what had to be done, one of them saying words.

The words finished, Bill grabbed the shovel and began filling in the grave. I took a turn for a while. The gravedigger stood, hunched over with cold, concentrating on being present. When the last of the earth was heaped up he took the shovel and patted the little mound tenderly, making sure it looked nice. I was glad he was there. His presence seemed to make it more of a service. We left the grave side then and Bill and I went to tell Peggy what we had done.

CHAPTER 9

A Deal's a Deal

The event may not be recorded in the annals of church history, for in truth, it caused only a light breeze of wonderment to pass through the parish at Battle Heights, the faith of the membership being sufficiently pliant to encompass minor, modern miracles. It was never noted on the long, blue pages of the annual congregational report. Yet, what happened on that particular Sunday was registered for ever in my memory and I record it now for posterity, because the day that Jim Parker came to church marked a triumph of evangelistic cunning on my part. While it is probably open to debate whether or not it did Jim any "good"—whether the Kingdom of God was thereby advanced—my budding ecclesiastical ego certainly got a substantial boost when he showed up, for Jim Parker, at least at that period in his life, was definitely not a church-goer.

Jim was clearly out of his element in church. Bouncing around on a John Deere tractor with a flock of Franklin's gulls wheeling behind his cultivator suited him well. He was at ease when his muscular body was engaged in the decisive rhythm of splitting firewood, or pitching bales of hay, or rounding up cattle. Essentially an outdoors man, he could tolerate the confines of the Empress Hotel beer parlour in Carrot River when absolutely necessary to quench his thirst, and since he worked hard, he was usually absolutely thirsty upon getting to town. But church? Never have I seen discomfort like the spectacle of Jim's six-foot-two frame folded into a grade three desk. Never has psychic pain been more visibly registered than on his tense countenance as he sat, bolt upright, directly below the stained plywood lectern that rested on the teacher's desk, enduring the drudgery of the sparse United Church Order of Service.

Bearing in mind that Protestant religion is second only to Catholicism in its ability to inculcate needless guilt, it will not be surprising to learn that, in spite of the lofty aim of my mission, as I delivered the "Call to Worship" on that fateful Sunday, I felt a twinge of remorse at having inveigled Jim's attendance, for he seemed like a mighty eagle trapped in a cage, resigned, unable to spread its wings. Still, a deal's a deal. I had delivered on my side of the bargain and now that he was paying up I was not about to release him until I administered a full dose of religion.

It all went back to the night of the dance. When word went out that a dance was to be held in Glen Horn school at Battle Heights, bachelors and belles, husbands and wives, families including infants in arms, children and oldsters, drained out of the territory at the close of the working day and drifted towards the one-room school situated a mile east of Barney Thiessen's store. It was an event I didn't want to miss. Quite apart from the opportunity to show community interest and to mingle with parishioners, I was no Methodist. I danced, and liked it.

Dances at Battle Heights had a reputation reaching back twenty years to the early days of settlement. The eyes of older raconteurs would sometimes glisten and a smug smile would ignite at recollections of nights gone bye when limbs were more supple and stomach linings were tougher.

One dance in particular was often the subject of sweet nostalgia. In the summer of 1939 the Germain boys, who had a lively family band called "The Lucky Moon Four," decided to build a dance hall east of Bill's Store. Before the roof was finished they held the first and only dance ever to pound its fancy floor. By all accounts it was a spectacular event, extending well into the wee hours. Next morning it started to rain, and since the roof was unfinished, the floor got soaked. That was a wet summer, and the floor never did dry out. It buckled and warped, and the building had to be torn down. Then war broke out. The Germain brothers moved away and were never heard from again. Nevertheless, the community's renown for good dances held through the years and a hoedown at Battle Heights was sure to attract people from far and wide.

Things didn't get under way till ten-thirty or eleven o'clock in the evening, for there were chores to do, pretty dresses to press with irons heated on the kitchen stove, last minute patches to be sewed onto scrubbed dungarees, and Dubbin to be lathered onto scraped boots. Women had piles of sandwiches and fancy baking to prepare, while quite a few of the men had flasks to fill from caches in the hay mow or the woodshed. It was around ten o'clock, when Charlie drove Mary and the girls over to the school with trays of food. Jim left on his own to meet some of "the boys" beforehand. I stayed behind to put the finishing touches to my sermon for next morning, then I too headed for the dance.

The land was red rimmed with northern sunset as I drove west towards the school. I geared down well ahead of the rickety bridge spanning the ditch, eased into the schoolyard and slid the Model A among the pickup trucks already parked there. Gathered about the open door of the school, but disappearing in twos and threes around the corner of the building from time to time, stood a pack of young men whose conversation limped to a lull as I came forward. I didn't recognize any of them, but trusting in western friendliness, I approached.

"Hi," I greeted as I took up a position at the edge of one of the several knots making up the group. In response I got a few nods and a couple of grudging grunts. Not to be daunted, I pressed on with cordiality.

"Nice evening for the dance." This managed to elicit some agreeable "yeps," but it also drew the pugnacious wit of a couple of young fellows standing further back, who weren't bothering to go behind the building, but who were openly swigging from bottles of beer. Loud enough to make sure I heard, one of them mimicked the rhythm of my words.

"Nya-dada-da-da-da," he minced, and their duet of snickers was washed down with slugs of beer.

"Where the hell'd he come from?" one asked the other, rhetorically.

"I dunno. Maybe we s'd find out."

"Yea. And send 'im back where he belongs." More snickers. More gulps of beer. With a sense of déjà vu I recognized all the elements. The boys were looking for a rumble.

Now, my spiritual convictions were sincere. I was devoted to the Gospel of love and peace. I believed profoundly in "turning the other cheek." It made a wonderful text to preach on. Trouble was, even with several opportunities to the good, I had never been able to abide by it. The society in which I grew up as a lad in Northern Ireland was, unfortunately, devoid of role models in backing down. From the age of fifteen till entering college at twenty-two, I had worked in the rough and tumble of building construction, and for the past two years in college I had been involved in boxing as a sport. I didn't feel pugnacious and I was sure I didn't portray the image of a scrapper. However, I also knew that whatever my multitudinous inaptitudes may have been, they were not in the area of fending for myself if necessary. This was a very un-ecclesiastical characteristic, yet, there it was.

A couple of farm lads fuelled with beer was no cause for alarm. In fact, if truth were known, a delightful surge of adrenalin was already coursing through my veins. My mantle of Christianity was genuine, it was just thin in places, and beneath the surface stirred some ancient Irish, Druid inclinations. I wasn't afraid of the fellows with the beer-loose tongues, but I worried that my own un-ministerial background would come untied, and that I would allow myself to be goaded into something that would bring disgrace to the Church, distress to the people of the parish, and discredit to myself as a candidate fit for the ministry. Yet, something had to be done.

Knowing that the one who gets in the first blow is often at a tremendous advantage in these situations, I decided to make my move swiftly.

"Hi," I said stepping towards the duo. "You boys sound like you're having a good time. I don't believe we've met. My name's Hugh, I'm the student minister here. I'm pleased to meet you." I lathered them each with a warm smile and extended a friendly hand. Before they knew what they were doing they had each shaken hands with me. Maintaining the warm smile I looked each of them directly in the eye and put resolve into the handshake.

While this was going on a couple of pickups had swung into the yard. From one of them strode the strapping figure of big Jim Parker.

"Hi Hugh," he said, slapping me an affectionate whack on the shoulder. "Good t'see ya. What's goin on?" he asked, glancing around the group.

"Oh, I was just getting acquainted with some of the boys here," I said. From that moment everyone was a lot more friendly. Nobody messed with Jim Parker.

The two young fellows, who weren't from Battle Heights, soon took off. I hung around the door for a while, listening to chat about crops, enjoying the banter, and even though I didn't recognize any of them, listening, enthralled, to the litany of names when somebody enquired, "Who's in there?" which was another way of asking what girls had shown up.

Delegations kept breaking off the main throng to disappear around the side of the school for short periods, and after a while, Jim fixed me with deliberate gaze, a faint smile lighting his features as he tilted his head in the direction of the corner of the building. "Are ya gonna have a little drink, Hugh. S'nothin' sayin' a student minister can't have a drink, ya know."

"Oh, I don't think so, Jim. Anyway, I'm going in to get a few dances before you guys come and take over all the good looking women."

"Ya'd dance a whole lot better if ya had a little drink," Jim threw after me as I turned to go in the door. I waved him off with a chuckle and headed into the school, leaving a chorus of good-natured guffaw around the steps.

Inside, a fox trot was under way. Cramped into the northwest corner of the room an orchestra consisting of banjo, piano, and fiddle, picked, pounded, and sawed a rhythmic and repetitious tune that sailed forth in perpetual search of its own elusive ending, the piano laying down blocks of no-nonsense chords over which the banjo and fiddle plunked and whipped their individual understandings of the melody. Meanwhile a whirlpool of people eddied about the room: farm-hands with earnest concentration on their sun-bronzed faces ("All ya gotta do is count the damn beats"), teenage girls, swirling beneath their partners' upraised arms to show off new frocks made to patterns picked from pictures in Eaton's catalogue; mountainous men with broad suspenders over clean shirts, feigning indifference to the whereabouts of their furtive feet; stout women tugging down dresses that had mysteriously shrunk since last dance; little girls beaming new-toothed grins while dancing with their daddies; pubescent boys with rebellious hair disciplined with Vaseline Hair Tonic from Barney's store, acting "real cool" with the neighbour girl from down the road; and joining the tide, the student minister, yanked to the floor by shy Sheila, who was dared to ask by her sister. Sheila was giggling now with embarrassment, bashful at sudden closeness with the young man from the East whose lips said, "let us pray" on Sundays, but who at this moment was thinking how pretty she looked. At last, the music straggled to an uneven finish and we all, like flotsam, landed back at the desks along the walls.

A wave of conversation filled in behind the receding tide of music. Explosions of laughter filled the hall while brows were mopped and faces fanned. At the back of the room huge kettles of coffee and tea were being boiled on a bank of camp stoves, while an army of women put last-minute touches to tables laden with tea-towel-veiled sandwiches and goodies that would be served for lunch sometime after midnight. I was about to cruise around the room to chat with people I recognized when the activity began again.

"Grab your partners everybody. Grab your partners for a square dance," yelled the caller, and the orchestra gave a brief burst of spirited music to rouse people from the desks. "That's it. Eeeeverybody up. Heeere we go." The caller was a short wisp of a man but he had powerful batteries. His voice belted out over the din. "One more couple. We need 'nother couple up here. One more couple, right here. That's it. Another couple needed over there with Stan and Nel. How're ya doin back there, Jack?"

"We need two more," yelled Jack McEwen, supported by the others in his group who had hands up, two fingers waving in the air.

"Two more back there in the corner," boomed the caller.

I watched as the couples grouped—four pairs to a square, ladies to the left of their partners, head couples with their backs to the music. I would like to have joined in but felt inadequate, for although I knew the basics, I was afraid I wouldn't know the steps of the particular dances. Besides, as soon as word reached "the outside world" that it was time for a square dance, there was a sudden influx of men and a corresponding depletion of eligible young women along the desk-lined walls.

"Hey, Hugh." I heard my name in the confusion. "Come on, get up here." Stan and Nelly Wilson were waving me into their square that still lacked one couple. Before I had time to reply Nelly came and pulled me into place by the hand while Stan sashayed off to the other side of the room to find a partner for me. I don't believe he put a whole lot of thought into the task, but in his defence, there wasn't much time, nor choice for that matter, and if it had been left to my own usual hesitant pace in things of this nature the dance would have been long over before I managed to get a partner. In a moment Stan was back, towing a reluctant young woman of ample proportions, whom he deposited beside me, a grin of great pride and accomplishment on his face. My partner and I had just enough time to say hello when the music burst over us and the caller's resonant voice rang out.

"Honour your corners. Bow to your own.
Allemande left and come back home."

My partner's apparent diffidence disappeared at the first strain of music. She sprang to life with surprising agility for her size and with obvious confidence. So did the whole hall. Left hand over right hand, over left, the circles threaded. Intertwining people-chains.

"Swing your partners one and all."

My partner seized and swung me. This was the first inkling I had that I might be in some sort of mortal danger. We got the hold right—left hands clasped at mid-body, her right hand on my left shoulder, my right hand firmly planted in the small of her back, which in fact wasn't at all small. I was proud that I had learned the right way to square dance swing at the Y.M.C.A. in London, Ontario. But, of course, in retrospect, I had never really swung before. Not really. I swung now. Using her substantial weight to advantage, my partner simply planted herself in one spot and pivoted as my body circumscribed patterns around her, my thrashing feet hitting the floor only occasionally. I thought, "If she ever lets go I'm done for."

"Then promenade around the hall."

She let go. Carried by unbridled centrifugal force, I went spinning into space. Just when I was about to leave the earth's atmosphere, I was yanked back by a sudden, socket-rending jerk. She hadn't let go after all, or else she had caught my desperately extended arm at the last moment. I snapped back to her embrace like a sprung garter. She turned me in the right direction and we promenaded.

The floor swirled with multi-coloured human cartwheels. Spirited "whoops" and "yahoooos" pierced the music. Skirts flounced and feet flashed, and heavy, half-laced work boots shuffled and stomped in thunderous rhythm till the building vibrated, and the cracks between the floor boards yielded up years of dried mud that filled the room with a brown haze of dust.

Relentlessly the music drove on. The caller's sturdy voice barked out the moves, "do sa do . . . allemande left. . . . grand chain . . . promenade. . . . dip 'n dive. . . . swing. . . ." When it came to swinging, my partner was a powerful woman. I learned to brace myself, and though disaster was never far away, I did manage to stay closer to the surface of the earth. Orientation was sometimes a problem coming out of one of these spins, and on one occasion I found myself in the wrong square, which set up an interesting group dynamic, for I was swiftly pushed, prodded, and pulled back to my own group. The frenzy rose and it seemed the little schoolhouse would surely burst at the seams till at last, holding hands, the dancers surged to the centre of their circles with a resounding, "wheeeee," then out, and back again, "wheeeee," and once again, "wheeeee."

The music stopped only long enough to allow the orchestra members to take a few swigs from suspicious bottles of pop before starting anew, for square dances were done in sets of three. "Turkey in The Straw" and "Birdie in the Cage" were yet to come.

By the end of the third dance the temperature in the schoolhouse was like a sauna, and it looked like a prairie dust storm had been stirred up within its walls. The windows had been opened, allowing mosquitos to find targets on the backs of sweaty necks. I decided to get outside for a breath of fresh air and perhaps to spit out a brick or two of dust.

Just as there had been an influx at the beginning of the square dance, there now was a general exodus of men. Jim was among them and it wasn't long till he was again suggesting that I ought to join him and his friends for a drink.

"Wouldn't hurt to have one just to be sociable, ya know," he argued.

"I'll tell you what," said I. "I'll take a drink with you if you'll come to church on Sunday." I reckoned that would put an end to the discussion, and sure enough the suggestion seemed to stop Jim in his tracks for a while. For a few seconds he had a somewhat stunned look on his face, as though calculating the cost and concluding the price was too high. But, to my surprise his face suddenly lit into a grin.

"O.K. It's a deal." We shook on it and headed around the corner of the building.

There, on the dark side of the schoolhouse, a little circle of "the boys," consisting of four pioneer farmers and the student minister, performed one of Canada's best established and most cherished rituals. I paid close attention, for there seemed to be a definite protocol to the way things had to be done, and later research confirms that the ritual is fairly universal.

The first drinker unscrewed the top and threw it away. This removed any danger of the drinking ending before the bottle was finished. Then, with a perfunctory toast to everybody's health, the bottle was hoisted and tipped back, the drinker allowing conspicuous air bubbles to gurgle through the neck before ending the "pull" and exclaiming, "Ahaaa, that's good stuff," wiping his mouth with the back of his hand and passing the bottle on. The next member of the circle assumed an air of no great urgency. He followed standard hygiene by wiping the top of the bottle with the palm of the hand, saving the back of the hand for his mouth, later. This was carried out in a casual, unconscious manner while telling us how sow-thistle had got into his summer fallow, and how it was "a bugger to get rid of," to which everyone, including my farm-knowledgable self, agreed, which seemed to be a good time to tilt the bottle.

When it came my turn to wipe the top of the bottle I thought of rendering a short summary of Sunday's sermon, but I knew none of them had been drinking enough to agree to that, so I just went ahead and took my swig. I have no idea what was in that bottle. Since everyone else seemed to agree that it was "good stuff," I didn't have the nerve to ask, but to my unseasoned palate it was like swallowing a Christmas tree, backwards. I made sure not to cough and splutter, though I believe I lost my voice for a while and my eyes filled with tears. All in the interest of gathering souls to the bosom of the Church, I remained for another round, whereupon I reminded Jim of his side of the bargain, went back to the dance, searched out my previous partner and swung her around the hall like she had never been swung before.

That's how Jim Parker came to be in church a couple of

Sundays later. He found it impossible to bow his head in the prayer and almost impossible not to do so during the sermon, but he was there, an honourable man, keeping his side of the bargain. I liked Jim a lot. I think he liked me too. He came to church again on my last Sunday in the community. And I hadn't even had another drink.

Hugh McKervill, student minister.

Main Street, Carrot River, Saskatchewan, 1955.

Bill's Store, 1955. Photo: Stan Wilson.

Bill's Store now. Photo: Hugh W. McKervill.

Peggy Kowalsky, 1956. Photo: Marjorie Brown.

Don, Nelly, and Stan Wilson at Glen Horne school, Battle Heights.

Alfred Sauder, Gordie Rowan, Bud Kowalsky,
and Gordon Rowan hauling mail.

The mud could suck the mightiest machine into its grip.
Photo: Tom Derry.

Spring flood at the bridge over the Carrot River between Battle Heights and Smoky Burn. Photo: Barney Thiessen.

Flooded river flats looking east on road from Battle Heights to Smoky Burn. Photo: Stan Wilson.

Alfred Sauder and Bud Kowalsky taking mail to Smoky Burn in a homemade boat during spring flooding. Photo: Stan Wilson.

Stan's garage on a wet spring day.

Smoky Burn schoolhouse and teacherage during a wet spring.
Photo: Duff and Lorna Watts.

Battle Heights schoolhouse ready for church. Photo: Stan Wilson.

*Student minister, caravaners, and vacation Bible school
children at Battle Heights, 1956.*

Feeding Gumbo.

CHAPTER 10

Shem

On those rare occasions when the roads were thoroughly dry, thus providing little excuse for getting stuck in the mud, the Model A would frequently find some other excuse to become immobile, even if it was something as mundane as a flat tire. It was on such an occasion that I first met Shem.

Travelling west from Smoky Burn towards Battle Heights one sunny day, my spirits were high. The road was hard, the sky was blue, and the Model A was putting roadside magpies to flight at a speed that belied its years. The river was summer docile as I crossed the iron-frame bridge and sped along the flats. As usual, the car complained and slowed down climbing the slope from the river valley, but it began picking up the pace again once back on the level.

Here the road passed through tall spruce and poplar before emerging into cleared land at the eastern extremities of Battle Heights, with wheat, oats, and rye growing between windrows. The Model A was still wheezing when I spied three figures walking on the road a couple of hundred yards ahead. They seemed to have simply materialized, and I wondered if they had emerged from the woods. As the distance decreased I could see they were Indian people. They turned around when they heard the car, and stuck out their thumbs in a hitch-hiking sign.

Immediately, I activated the elaborate routine required to bring the Model A to a stop. I geared down to second, pressed the brake pedal to the floor, geared down into first, hauled back on the emergency brake, made myself rigid against the useless foot brake again, and waited.

The faith of the three Indian men in automotive technology was touching, if ill-placed, for none of them had bothered to move from the centre of the road, and when I took to waving them away through the open window they mistook my intent and waved back. It was a great relief when the Model A finally came to rest inches from the closest of them. They were fellows about my own age dressed in jeans and tattered jackets. The sun glinted off their black hair, and their broad copper countenances broke into grins as they slowly approached the driver's window.

"Hi," said one of them, the other two staying a little back.

"Hi," I replied.

"Nice car you got there," said the spokesman, soft voiced. One of the others said something in his own language and the three of them burst into schoolboyish snickers.

"Oh, it gets me around, most of the time. You guys looking for a ride?" I asked.

"Maybe," came the reply. "Maybe w'll go with you to Barney's." I hadn't intended going as far as the store, but it wouldn't be much out of my way.

"Sure, I can take you to the store. Hop in," I said, and the three of them clambered to the passenger door and began turning and tugging at the handle, breaking into renewed laughter when the door wouldn't open. Between their tugging and my kicking from the inside, the door finally flew open and the three of them piled in, two in the back and the one who had done the talking beside me in the front. He slammed the door and it bounced back open. This caused a new outburst of laughter. For an instant I felt annoyed that these fellows who were begging a ride were laughing at the vehicle providing it. Yet, there was no "put down" in their manner. They were simply and genuinely amused. Indeed, I found their guileless good humour infectious and soon joined in laughing with them.

"You have to jiggle the handle," I instructed. The word "jiggle" touched off a whole new wave of mirth. The two who had not spoken to me spluttered something in their own language, with the word "jiggle" standing out like a landmark in, what was to me, an incomprehensible word-wilderness. I wondered if the word was close to one in their own language, or did the sound simply amuse them? I never found out. However, after much jiggling and giggling, we got under way.

Once we got rolling I felt compelled to converse. It was my first encounter with Indian people and I was anxious to learn all I could about them, and as all good white liberals do, to let them know that I wasn't prejudiced, which of course, like all good white liberals, I was. As I was to discover through personal experience later in life, the dialogue that occurred in the Model A was typical of most attempts at communication between Indian people and other Canadians. I did a lot of talking and asked a lot of questions. The three hitchhikers said "Yeah" a lot and laughed easily, but mostly they wrapped themselves in protective, expressionless silence.

"I'm the student minister around here. My name's Hugh."

"Yeah—ha ha. Hi." I waited for more. Nothing.

"What're your names?" The one in the front told the names of the back-seat occupants who sat silently and, as I could see in the rearview mirror, with faces completely devoid of expression. When they heard their names mentioned they both responded by saying "Hi" again. I have forgotten their names, for apart from this repeated greeting, they didn't speak to me and I never saw them again after that day.

"They don't speak English," said my front-seat passenger, as though reading my mind. Maybe not, but they seemed to understand quite well, I thought, for when it suited them, they responded to the conversation, usually by laughing.

"And what's your name," I persisted.

"Shem."

"Shem." I repeated. "Like in the Bible? That's a good name."

"Yeah—ha ha ha," said Shem, looking straight ahead. "I know."

". . . Noah became the father of Shem," I thought, remembering the text in Genesis. I wondered how much he knew about the origin of his name. It was a name that evoked images of missionary influence, of superimposed Judaeo-Christian culture. It said nothing of his own cultural roots. There was a moment of silence as some disturbing thoughts raced through my mind.

"So, where are you guys from?"

"Red Earth," replied Shem, without embellishment. Red Earth was a Cree Indian reserve with, at that time, a population of approximately 370 people. It lay between the Carrot River and Red Earth Lake, a good twenty miles east of Smoky Burn along a foot trail through the forest, almost twice as far by wagon trail. I had picked up this much information from some of the settlers, but I wanted to draw Shem and his pals out. So I asked:

"Where is Red Earth from here anyway?"

"Back that way," said Shem, nodding back over his shoulder.

"How far would that be?"

"Pretty far. Yeah—ha ha—long way."

"So, how did you get here. Did you walk?" I asked.

"Yeah, walk. Mostly. But sometimes we come the long way with the horses."

"Boy! That's a long walk."

"Yeah, long walk. Maybe twenty miles." It was actually more like twenty-five or six to where I had picked them up. A marathon. They did it all the time, coming out to find day work picking roots and rocks off newly broken land for the settlers, sleeping in granaries, camping at the side of the road, or congregating on the small piece of land that Bill Boschman had set aside for their use beside the store, a tradition upheld by Barney and Anne. I learned that the trio had already been working around Battle Heights. They had left their gear at the camp beside the store and walked back to the reserve to see their wives for a couple of days, a round trip of sixty miles by foot. On the way back they had broken the journey by stopping in Smoky Burn to sleep in a granary.

Just then, the car gave a sudden lurch, followed by the telltale flop-flop-flop of a flat tire. A blow out. The vehicle wobbled to a stop, and after the usual rigmarole to get out, the four of us stood looking at the damage: a flat, rear, left wheel. Needless to say, my passengers found the spectacle extremely funny. I was constitutionally unable to see anything to laugh about. In fact, it was downright annoying to have them standing around snickering, because the nuisance was greater than they realized.

With prophetic foresight, the Church had made sure that the Model A was equipped with a spare tire. It was mounted on the rear of the vehicle where it gave a finished look to the otherwise bare back end. Care had also been taken to ensure that a wheel wrench was stored under the front seat. Unfortunately, that's as far as preparedness went. There was no jack, and on a lonely, mud road in northern Saskatchewan this lacuna rendered the first two precautionary provisions more or less irrelevant.

I understood this to be a deliberate arrangement tied into the essentials of Christian theology, because in much Biblical research and doctrinal scholarship there exists what is known as "the missing link," which, of course, cannot be said with certainty to actually exist, because it is always missing. In the gap left by the missing link, faith is expected to take over. Obviously, it would not have been appropriate to have sent a student minister to the Canadian frontier without a "missing link." His faith might have languished for lack of exercise.

While I was contemplating this ontological situation, two things happened. First, the mosquitos and blackflies found me. I say "me" because they were in a cloud around my head, no doubt delirious at their good fortune, and I was flapping frantically at them, while my passengers seemed to be relatively unperturbed, casually crushing the most annoying ones without expending much energy.

The second thing that happened was that the hitchhikers took off. I had just explained the theory of the "missing link," as it pertained to the Model A. Shem responded by summing it all up. "No jack eh. Ha-ha-ha." The three of them conversed for a moment in Cree, had another good laugh, then simply left. They slid down the ditch, leapt across the trickle of water, climbed up the other side and disappeared into the woods. The mosquitos and blackflies stayed behind with me.

I heard the deserters crashing about in the woods, which had been partially logged and were full of slash. "So much for the stealthy Native slinking through the primal forest," I thought. Meantime, I had to decide what to do. It was not inconceivable that no traffic would pass this way for a full day or more. At best, it could be hours before a vehicle might come from either direction. I would have to walk, but I had no intention of following the three Indian lads. I couldn't see how the direction they had gone would get them to the store any faster than by using the road. I tied the car door shut and started walking. Walking, flapping, and slapping. It was clear that the mosquitos and blackflies were not going to stick with the car.

I had gone only a few steps when a huge chunk of log came flying out of the forest, followed by another and another. Then the three Indian fellows came out dragging a long pole, picking up the pieces of log and throwing them ahead again and again till all the pieces were across the ditch and beside the car. With efficiency of movement, they stacked short logs behind the rear wheel. Then they slid the long poplar pole over the pile of logs and under the axle. Using their bodies as weight they levered the rear of the car sufficiently for me to slide a chunk of log under the axle, whereupon I changed the tire with the speed of a grand prix pit-stop mechanic. We threw the chunks of wood back across the ditch and were soon on our way again, leaving behind a storm of furious mosquitos, though, to use language still employed by one of my minister friends, "a goodly number" came with us inside the car. Inside me, I was humbly rearranging some of my opinions about the three passengers.

As we got close to Battle Heights corner it was Shem who broke the silence. "Pretty thirsty." He said, reflectively.

"Yeah, I'm pretty thirsty myself," I said. Shem was looking contemplatively out the window at the passing fields of young wheat. Then he looked sideways at me and said, with a mischievous grin,

"Indians like too much pop. 'Sno good for our teeth." I didn't know what to say in response. There was a long silence. Before I could think of something appropriate, he went on, wistfully, "But, I like it anyway."

"Well, I suppose most things are o.k. in moderation," I said. Inwardly, I cringed and thought, "Jeeze, I sound like a white preacher." Shem spoke up again.

"Trouble is, I got no money. My friends, they got no money neither." I could see now where he was heading. I said nothing, waiting. "Maybe I'll borrow a coupla bucks offa you," said Shem. I glanced toward him. He was grinning from ear to ear, as though this bright idea had just occurred to him.

We were at Battle Heights now and I wheeled into the yard at Stan's garage to get the tire repaired. I had a total of one dollar and fifty-seven cents in my pocket, which I gave to Shem. "Thanks," he said, and the three of them ran and skipped across the road to Barney's place. They emerged a little later, loaded with soft drinks, chocolate bars, and penny candies. With pop at seven cents a bottle and chocolate bars five cents each, they had done well. Shem was having a hard time balancing his purchases, because he had two bottles of pop, one in each hand, and he was trying to unwrap a chocolate bar at the same time. He broke away from the other lads and ambled across the road towards Stan's place, where I was pretending not to be in a hurry to get the tire repaired. "Here," he said, thrusting a bottle of Coke towards me. "I knew you was thirsty, so I bought you pop."

I didn't see Shem again that summer till the week I was to return to college. I had pulled into Stan's place to chat with him about work that should be done on the Model A over the winter. Recognizing the car, Shem came running across the road from the Indian camp beside the store. He was grinning broadly, and I had the feeling he was glad to see me. "Hi," he greeted. "I pay you back now," was the first thing he said, and he handed me one dollar and fifty-seven cents. I told him that I really didn't expect him to pay it back, and that, anyway, he had helped me with the flat tire. But he insisted, and in the end I took it. We chatted for a while. He had "lotsa work pickin' roots" that summer. I told him I was going back to college soon. "Yeah—ha ha ha," he responded, the laugh feeble. " 's pretty far, uh?"

"Yeah. Its a long way. Too far to walk, Shem."

"Yeah. Too far."

"Come on. Let me buy you a pop," I said.

"Yeah, ha-ha-ha, o.k." We walked across to Barney's together, drank pop and parted, each to our own world.

CHAPTER 11

I Came Back

When I left the area in September 1955, I had no intention of ever setting foot in Saskatchewan gumbo again. It had been an interesting experience, but I was lonely for pavement. I liked most of the people, but I was anxious to see my own family and friends. During the next winter at Waterloo College I planned with a fellow pre-theology student to spend the following summer, after graduation, hitchhiking around Europe. It was the thing to do. One day in late winter, however, I received a letter from the Home Missions Board telling me that the people of Smoky Burn, Papikwan, and Battle Heights had written to the Board requesting that, if possible, I be sent back for a second term. The Church wished to know if I would be interested in returning. I was touched. The European tour was cancelled, and in lieu of sidewalk cafes and cathedrals I returned to mud, mosquitos, and schoolhouses. This time I brought my rubber boots and was successful in forgetting the hat.

It had been agreed between the communities that the student minister would be stationed in Battle Heights and Smoky Burn on alternate years. Consequently, during my second sojourn I stayed at Smoky Burn, housed alone in a ten by fourteen foot shack situated on the southwest corner of the Kowalsky farm, about half a mile east of the school and the co-op store.

The structure's principal advantage as a manse was that during heavy rain it didn't leak—much. The water stains on the unpainted wallboard revealed previous tide marks that had come up through the floor in spring rather than down through the roof. Its most immediate disadvantage was that it was already occupied by an industrious and prolific family of mice whose traces were to be found in great quantities on every horizontal surface, along with shovelfuls of dead flies. I also had to share the space with two dozen limp cardboard boxes filled with assorted paraphernalia: winter clothing, machine parts, worn through rubber boots, broken kerosene lamps, an array of used paint cans complete with uncleaned brushes in various stages of rigor mortis. There were other sundry items temporarily set aside from the mainstream of daily use, though not condemned, for in this country nothing was discarded lightly.

I evicted the mice easily enough by kidnapping one of the Kowalsky barn cats and keeping it hostage for a while. It turned out to be more trouble than the mice, however, and I was happy to release it after only a few days. Once the shovelling and sweeping and scrubbing were done, and the boxes were piled in corners, there was room to move between the wood range and the round, oak dining-room table with its two chairs. Against the south wall, beside the door, stood a tall kitchen cabinet that must have been a haughty piece of furniture at one time, but it had been shamed with innumerable coats of unseemly paint, the latest being garish yellow. It was filled with junk that had nothing to do with kitchens, and which I redistributed into the cardboard boxes to make room for peanut butter, jam, sardines, and beans. The back six feet of the cabin was partitioned off into a sleeping area. A moth-eaten curtain formed a doorway into this dark sanctum where I spent the nights on a narrow cot, sensing vague loneliness, listening to the haunting howls of timber wolves.

I missed the comfort and companionship of boarding with

the Parkers. I also savoured the solitude and would often stay up late, reading, studying, writing, aware of the vast northern night around me, a pot of tea distilling into pure tannic acid on the wood range, the hissing gas lantern keeping me company. On such a night, when all was still save for the slumping coals in the wood range, I was just thinking of getting ready for bed when a knock on the door sent me almost through the roof. Hesitantly, I opened the door. There stood Shem, the light from the lantern illuminating his bronze features.

"Hi. I come to visit you," was all he said.

"Visit, at twelve-thirty in the morning?" I thought. But what I said was: "Hi. Come on in. It's good to see you." He came in, dragging a light pack and bedroll that he set in a corner against some boxes. Then he flopped into a chair. He looked dishevelled. I noted blood matted at the fringe of his hair—the work of blackflies and no-see-ums. He wore jeans, a plaid shirt, and a light jacket with the pocket torn. On his feet were black canvas runners, soaked and muddy, with no socks. He smelt like a mixture of bread dough and wet wood ashes. He was obviously exhausted, and I knew without asking that he had just walked the twenty miles through the forest from Red Earth. He sat with his legs apart, his forearms resting on his thighs, and his head hanging like a tired pack horse.

"Are you hungry, Shem?" I asked.

"Yeah. Pretty hungry."

"I'll make you something to eat," I said, and pushed some dry wood into the firebox. The teapot was still on the side of the stove and I poured him a cup, stirring in three spoons of sugar without asking. "Do you like milk?"

"Yeah. I like it." I shoved the can of Carnation across the table towards him.

"There. Help yourself," I said, and set about opening a can of beans and tossing bread on top of the stove to toast. I put the kettle on for more tea. In the tall cabinet there was a chunk of home-cured bacon and a couple of eggs that Peggy Kowalsky had given me for breakfast, so I fried these while the beans, for want of a pot, were heating in the can. When it was all ready I served Shem a mountainous portion, took some beans and toast myself, and we sat at the table and ate. We didn't talk.

After eating we turned our chairs from the table and faced the range so we could stare at the red coals in the firebox and sip more tea. I was determined to adapt to Shem's pace of conversation, which meant we were silent most of the time. At first I found this difficult. I was conscious of the quietness. The lantern hiss, the muffled splutters of wood burning in the stove, and the purring of the kettle were the only sounds.

For a while, I had an almost uncontrollable urge to fill the gaps with words. Gradually, however, I became more comfortable. I began to understand that for Shem, visiting was a matter of being present with the other. It occurred to me that in my own cultural tradition, words, which are supposed to be instruments of communication, are often the very means by which the possibility of intimacy is staved off. We build word walls to protect the self from closeness, then wonder why we are lonely. We engage in noisy barrages of verbosity. We cannot hear the still small voice of the soul of our brother or sister for the din of our talking. Shem and I sat facing the stove, not talking. Visiting. I felt his presence.

After a long time Shem said he was tired and he wanted to go to bed. I invited him to lay out his bedroll in the cabin, but he wouldn't. A trace of smile emerged on his face as he glanced at me and said, "Indians always sleep in granary."

"Well, Shem, you don't have to. You are welcome to stay in here. It'll be much warmer," I said.

"Granary's good. I sleep good there," he said, as he lifted his pack and bedroll to leave. I felt badly that he thought he had to go out and sleep in an empty granary. The northern spring nights were cold. I tried again to persuade him to stay in the warmth of my cabin.

"You know you're welcome to stay."

"Yeah, ha-ha-I know. 'S too hot. Good night."

"Good night." He was gone when I got up in the morning.

I saw Shem quite a few times that summer. One day he showed up on horseback. It was a medium-sized palomino. He rode bareback with a rope nose-halter—no bit nor fancy leather reins here. I patted the horse's neck and after a while I asked Shem if he minded if I rode her. He slid off and said, "Go ahead."

The first problem was how to get on, for there was no saddle to clutch and no stirrups to climb into. Shem could see that I was stymied. He stood beside the horse, facing the rear, and made a stirrup with his hands by locking his fingers together. His hoist was a bit too vigorous, however, so that instead of landing on the horse's back I went slithering right over the other side and landed on the ground, looking up at the horse's undercarriage. Sheepishly I came around for another try. Shem was laughing his head off. He hadn't had this much fun since the flat tire.

The next try was more successful. I was surprised how high up it was, and how little there was to hold onto. Shem handed me the halter rope and I said, "Giddyup." Nothing happened. So I repeated the order, more authoritatively. "Giiiiddy-up." The horse tossed me a disdainful glance over its shoulder, but gave no indication of "giddying up." We were standing amid the scattered young poplar sprouting up around the shack. Shem told me to reach out and break off a small branch. No sooner did the horse hear the snap of the twig, than it took off at a smart walk. The sudden forward movement caught me by surprise and I almost fell off backwards, but by clutching the mane and gripping with my knees I managed to stay aboard. It was a long way up.

We walked to the pasture behind the Kowalsky yard. The horse stopped. It was a hot day and bomber-sized horseflies accompanied by speedier greenbottles and deer flies were buzzing around the horse's head and attacking its flanks. Its tail was swishing and its ears twitching in a constant effort to ward them off. Several times it tried to turn back to the meagre shade of the poplars and each time I wrestled its head towards the open pasture. The whole exercise was clearly against the horse's will.

With the switch of poplar I applied a mere suggestion of persuasion to the rump. The horse took off across the pasture at a gallop, its mane flying back into my face as I hugged with my legs and attempted to capture the rhythm of the mountain of resentful muscle beneath me. It was exhilarating. Here I was, a fearless pioneer missionary braving the open plains on an Indian pony. I wished I had a big hat. I was an intrepid frontiersman chasing down a herd of bison. I was a tough, tobacco-spitting, raw-hided son-of-a-gun . . . "Eeeee-yyyy-pes." I was sailing through the air, over the horse's head. The horse, who had suddenly had enough of this nonsense, was already cantering back to Shem and the meagre shade of the saplings. I watched from my vantage point on the ground, my face perilously close to a fresh, green cow pie covered with ginger flies.

Shem let me ride his horse several times and as time went on I got better at it, though I don't believe the horse ever enjoyed itself as much as I did. Mainly, though, it was evening when Shem would arrive. We would eat, drink tea, and sit and watch the fire. Visiting. In time, Shem told me more about himself and his people. He had spent a year in the tuberculosis sanatorium at Prince Albert. "That's where I learned to speak English so good," he told me. Many people from the reserve had been to the sanatorium. Many had died. There was little work on the reserve. He did some trapping and hunting. His wife made hide moccasins and jackets with fancy beadwork. In the summer he worked for the settlers when he could get work. He wanted to be a carpenter.

I grew comfortable with the quietness of our visits, being content to listen to what Shem wanted to tell me. One night, after a long silence, without taking his eyes off the glow in the firebox, he said, "Sometimes I drink too much." I didn't reply. Instead, I poked a stick into the fire. Sometimes when he came to visit he was in rough shape, like that first night, and I could smell the homebrew working its way out through his pores. "Yeah," he continued. "Way too much. S'no good."

I waited, then responded the only way I could think of at the time. I simply made an affirmative noise that I hoped would sound empathetic. Then my Presbyterianism got the better of me and I said something to the effect that too much alcohol wasn't good, which was stupid. He already knew that.

"Yeah. S'no good for Indians," he reflected.

"Too much is no good for any of us, Shem."

"Yeah. Specially for the Indians," he insisted.

"I know what you mean," I said. But I really didn't.

On our last evening together, we ate bacon and eggs, drank tea, and spent a lot of time visiting. Shem suddenly broke the silence. He didn't actually look at me and there was no particular burden of emotion in his voice. He just summed up in a matter of fact way what he experienced to be true. "You know," he said, pausing slightly, "you're my friend." Before I answered I thought of the thousands of miles and the continents of culture and circumstances that lay between us and yet how close we had grown.

"And you're my friend too, Shem," I replied, with a lump in my throat.

"Yea-ha-ha-ha. I know." he said, reaching for the tea pot. "Is there any more tea?"

My relationship with Bill and Peggy Kowalsky also developed

during the second summer when I lived in the shack on the corner of their property. I never tried to match their early rising, but the irrepressible zeal of the morning rooster followed by the clatter of milk pails or the convulsions of the tractor starting up, made sleeping-in sheer misery. Peggy's raucous yell across the yard or a knock on the door by one of the children often summoned me to breakfast before I could get my own fire going. I turned the separator for her and she fed me thick porridge lathered with the cream I had just taken off, and nest-warm eggs dropped into a greasy pan, and fried bread like back in Ireland, and coffee and chatter, and the children—Isabelle, John, Norman, and Patricia—clambering all over me. It was before we knew about cholesterol. It was wonderful.

Some mornings I got up and trudged directly to the field where Bill had already been working for a couple of hours, and I would take over disc cultivating long enough to let him go back to the house for breakfast. I helped him mend fences, repair the pig pen, chop wood, muck out the barn, and we grew to know each other pretty well.

Bill was a severe Christian at that time. I was probably at the zenith of my own religious convictions, being youthful and in possession of a faith as yet neither influenced by study nor tested by personal pain. Yet, I had the feeling that my preaching and devotion failed to go far enough for Bill. When a travelling evangelist pitched his tent somewhere around Melfort, Bill packed the family into the car and raced off to "Get a good dose of the Gospel," as he explained to me.

There was no laziness in Bill. A wiry, tempestuous man, he flung himself at work, with the consequence that he often broke machinery and lost precious time. What machinery he had was aging and, compared to the two co-operatives which had stuck together, he had little borrowing power for the purchase of new equipment. Furthermore, the land he had acquired after Pasquia Hills Co-op disbanded was poorly drained and the wet years made farming difficult, sometimes impossible. Still, he was a hard worker, and like all pioneers he was driven forward by hope.

Endless work and hardship were the common lot of all the families pioneering in this northeastern corner of Saskatchewan during those wet years. But, it always seemed to me that life for Bill and Peggy was extra hard. They certainly didn't need, nor deserve, the additional pain of losing a baby at birth. Yet I don't remember them complaining.

Like many of my parishioners, the Kowalskys seemed to appreciate my attempts at being their minister. They were off-handedly kind and generous to me. They shared whatever food was on their table. They also gave me rich memories of simple pleasures, like sitting on a block of firewood in the middle of the yard, surrounded by wood chips and chicken droppings, chipping river ice off a sawdusty chunk taken from the icehouse, and packing it with salt into the hand turned ice-cream maker, the excited children dancing about me with gleeful anticipation.

Along with many others in the community, Bill and Peggy helped train me for the ministry by strengthening my own faith in, and admiration for, hard working, common men and women with all their faults and frailties. It's just that Peggy being from Belfast, and what I had to do for her that first summer, gave us a special bond.

CHAPTER 12

Sinbustin'

For thirty years, from 1948 till 1978—by which time improved roads enabled anyone interested in attending church to drive into Carrot River—the United Church of Canada sent student ministers to the Battle Heights, Smoky Burn, and Papikwan mission charge. I was eighth and ninth in this succession of greenhorns, and the only appointee the people were ever foolhardy enough to invite for a second term. My return apparently put a permanent end to that practice.

Like those who came before and after me, I was called by a variety of names, some of them to my face. Ordinarily, I was "the student minister." I would approach a group of men working on a piece of machinery in a shed at one of the co-operative farms, or picking rocks and roots on newly broken land, and I would overhear one of them say, "Watch your gad-dammed language boys, here comes the student minister."

Some fellows were always trying to get a rise out of the student minister. Tom Derry had a habit of telling me lewd jokes at which he would go into paroxysms of laughter. He and Jack Stevenson, or "Jwack" to his peers, regularly referred to me as "the sky-pilot," "the Bible-thumper," "the pulpit-pounder," "the preacher-man," or "God's travelling salesman." The epithets were always good natured, for although I did occasionally run into hostility, generally speaking, a propri-etary affection towards the student minister existed throughout the communities, even among people who never came to church. If there had been a prize for coming up with the most novel title, however, I believe Jack McEwen would have won it.

Jack and Dolly McEwen had moved onto their land in Battle Heights in the spring of 1953, splashing through mud to get there and arriving in time to contend with some of the worst of the wet years. With two small boys, they lived in an unfinished shell of a house, half a mile east and one mile north of Mary and Charlie Parker. The road north to their place was impassable for weeks at a time, but Dolly was a faithful churchgoer, and if Jack was busy working on the back quarter and couldn't get away to drive them with the tractor, she would often trudge the two miles to the schoolhouse to attend a Sunday service, sometimes carrying three-year-old Bill while the older lad, John, trotted along beside.

Jack was a powerfully built man who pitted himself relentlessly against the stubborn clay and bad weather in his effort to carve a farm out of the wilderness. He seldom came to church. There was too much work to be done. One day, I decided to bring the church to him by offering to help him pick roots. The road was soft and badly rutted, so I drove as far as I could and walked the remainder of the way. Jack was just coming out of the house as I arrived. Dressed in dungarees, the peak of his grease-laden railway engineer's cap shading his eyes and a homemade cigarette hanging from the left side of his mouth, he stopped in his tracks upon seeing me.

"Well, I'll be damned." he exclaimed, fetching the cigarette from his lips. "Here comes the sinbuster." And the name stuck like the gumbo that adhered to our boots.

The art of "sinbustin'," or, as it was more properly known in Toronto, "the functions of ministry," relied heavily upon visitation. Churchly visitation is just plain visiting pumped up with an air of pastoral purpose. Throughout the history of the western world a lot of potential for genuine human encounter has been ruined by this sort of thing. At Battle Heights, Smoky

Burn, and Papikwan I enjoyed the people and, as it turned out, I had quite a few wonderful visits with them, but I never did like visitation as a formal part of my work.

It wasn't just fear of territorially minded dogs that put me off the task. It was something deeper. For one thing, being on the perpetrating side of a minister's visit made me every bit as uncomfortable as I had always been when the venerable Dr. Davey used to drop in to see how our souls were doing during my boyhood in Northern Ireland. There would be a scurry to switch on the electric heater in the otherwise unused front parlour, fragments of dust fluff flashing on the glowing element and filling the cold air with acrid incense. There, in rigid cordiality, we would sip tea from delicate china that none of us was otherwise allowed to go near, all the family members acting far more genteel than we otherwise were. After the weather and the football scores were dispensed with, Dr. Davey would take out his Bible and read at us, whereupon my mother and father would nod in stern accord with various verses, and I would do the same, taking cues from my dad, whose ability to look earnest I admired. My brother and sister, who were much younger, alternated between squirming and looking awe stricken.

You had to pay attention during one of these visitations. If you didn't you could get caught nodding assent when you were supposed to have your eyes squeezed shut. The reverend doctor would suddenly cast his countenance towards the cracks in the ceiling, and with his silky white locks shaking with gravity, he would draw the attention of The Almighty, Omnipotent, Omnipresent, Omniscient Creator of the Universe to the plight in our front parlour, requesting custom-designed blessings for each and every one of us by name. He asked that my father be rewarded with prosperity for his honest industry, that my mother be granted wisdom and grace, that my brother and sister grow up to honour their father and mother, and that I be delivered from the temptations of the flesh, which caused me no end of consternation. I was convinced that Dr. Davey must know something.

Now that I was on the delivery side, the very thought of official, pastoral visiting still triggered the playing of these "old tapes," bringing on painful tensions in my psyche. I didn't see why I should spread this form of social discomfort out here on the Canadian frontier. Still, it was part of the job, so I threw myself into it and tried to be as relaxed and natural as possible.

Visitation entailed crisscrossing the territory, drinking gallons of tea and coffee, and consuming great quantities of pie and oven-hot bread spread with homemade preserves and cow-fresh cream. As I applied myself, my skills in pastoral visiting developed rapidly. I soon became adept at hanging around till I was told, "You might as well stay for lunch," or if it was late afternoon it might be suggested, "Buck will be in from the fields soon. Why don't you stay for dinner?"

Not that any of the families had front parlours in which to endure a pastoral visit. Nor the time. I could call on women and children so long as I was prepared to put up with the confusion of little ones crying and clambering for attention, or the gnawing noise of a gas engine driving the washing machine outside the door, with a pailful of dirty diapers sitting on the step. Most of the houses were cramped and cluttered, with flies whizzing in and out. The kitchens were often steamy from boilers bubbling on wood stoves, preserving wild saskatoon berries picked in competition with the bears.

And yet, for all my inner tensions, and in spite of the obstacles, now and then, some deeply personal exchanges took place across the oilcloth altar of a kitchen table. A work-weary woman might expose her fatigue through tears, a wife would worry about her marriage, or a mother might express fear for the future. "I don't know what's going to happen to us if we don't get a crop again this year," was a common expression of anxiety. I didn't have any answers. I probably didn't even know the questions. But I listened, and maybe that helped. Occasionally, if it seemed welcome, I read a passage of scripture, and when I did, I was told more than once that the words brought some comfort. Balm for a hurting soul. Sometimes, I was asked to say a prayer. After the "amen," the usual response was a simple, "Thanks Hugh."

Visiting the men was another matter. Indeed, it was an issue which penetrated to the very heart of my own masculinity, for I was always painfully conscious that visiting was an effete occupation compared to the long hours of heavy labour put in by the men on the farms. I could never justify it to myself as real work. Consequently, pastoral visiting with the men often took the form of digging post holes, mucking out barns, burning windrows, rounding up cows for milking, or picking rocks and roots. If a weightier topic than the rocks we were lifting or the bales of hay we were pitching happened to come up, we talked about it, though the content was more likely to be political than religious.

This approach seemed to fit the territorial realities. It also contributed to the overall purpose of my mission in that, quite apart from offering a modicum of ministry to the people, one of the aims of the student mission field program was to provide the Church's neophyte ministers with experiential learning opportunities. Without actually joining the men in rock picking on a remote quarter of the River Bend Co-op farm, for example, I might never have learned how to boil eggs by placing them in a sock and lowering them into the tractor's radiator while the radiator honeycomb was blocked with a jacket and the engine was revved to raise the temperature. This is a practical piece of know-how without which no preacher should ever mount the steps of a pulpit.

Another example of indispensable ingenuity that every self respecting parson ought to have at his or her fingertips was demonstrated by Bill Hope of River Bend farm. One day Bill found himself working a piece of land a couple of miles south of the farm yard, with tobacco and papers in his pocket, but no matches. Only smokers, or possibly ex-smokers, will fully appreciate the urgency of a situation like this, I'm told. Bill was a resourceful chap. He gathered a few tufts of sow-thistle down, soaked the fluffy seeds with gas from the tractor's sediment bowl and, with the engine running, ignited the tinder, the cigarette, and his eyebrows with a loosened spark plug cable. The electric jolts caused him to jump about like a wounded jack-rabbit. Bill chain-smoked for the rest of that shift.

There are those who would argue that the connection between forking manure and spreading the gospel is tenable enough. On the other hand, I would be hard pressed to show that learning acquired while working alongside these frontier farmers had any direct application during my subsequent years of ministry. I was never called upon to boil eggs in the pulpit, and during the few years I was foolish enough to smoke cigarettes there was never a tractor available when I needed a light. I did, however, gain a mighty respect for those hard-working men.

In the spring of '56 pastoral visiting in Smoky Burn took a peculiar turn. Almost from the day of my return I ran into a spate of planned dinner invitations complete with specific dates and times. Initially, I saw this new trend as an attempt to bring order and predictability to bear upon my habit of dropping in unannounced. I even thought it might be the community's way of making sure I got proper meals, now that I was "baching" alone in the little hut. As time went on, however, I grew suspicious that an element of conspiracy was afoot, for wherever I went—and I never turned down an invitation—

the schoolteacher was always there. She was beginning to think that the student minister was ubiquitous.

This was Marjorie Stuckert's first job. For $1,900.00 a year, plus $200.00 isolation pay, she taught twenty-five children in grades one to nine, eight of them in grade one. She earned an additional fifteen dollars a month as janitor of the one-room schoolhouse, and paid the same amount back to the school board for rent of the teacherage. It was a two-room building situated behind the school, and was only slightly superior to my own accommodations.

Marjorie was well liked. She distinguished herself by being the first teacher to survive a full school year at Smoky Burn. Former incumbents either fled the discomforts or were picked off by marriage. Although I had met her briefly the previous fall I had failed to notice what had not been missed by a group of surveyors working on a drainage project a mile or so north of the school. Every noon, and again at 3:30 P.M., they trained the sights of their transit onto the door of the schoolhouse to torture themselves with a telescopic inspection of the teacher's finer features as she left the building.

When word of this reached my ears it awakened a primeval rutting instinct within me. Hitherto unsuspected charms seemed to emanate from the demure young teacher with the sandy hair and freckled face. With every passing day her looks improved. I reasoned with myself that, after all, we had a lot in common, she and I being the only people in the territory who didn't get dirty doing our jobs. It got so that the very prospect of Marjorie's presence at these dinner invitations provoked in me a whole new appreciation for visitation as an indispensable function of pastoral ministry, and I immediately set about broadcasting my hope to visit every family in the district.

I realized that taking advantage of my position like this was unfair competition so far as the surveyors were concerned.

Then again, they had their surveyor's instrument, and they had never invited me to take a peek through it. So, I redoubled my efforts. The community had never known such a cyclone of visitation as, unstintingly, I devoted myself to the duty of dining on plain but sturdy stews, steaks, and roasts of moose meat, elk, venison, and chicken, some of it probably hunted legally—particularly the chicken. And, almost everywhere I went that spring, Marjorie the schoolteacher was sure to be there.

As the conspiracy thickened, it was brought to my attention from time to time by a number of the Smoky Burn women that Marjorie Stuckert was from sound Saskatchewan farm stock, and that she baked a good loaf of bread. Spurred on by this crucial piece of intelligence, I pressed my advantage. I invited her for a late ride in the Model A to look at flecks of moonlight on the rapids up by Tom Derry's place. She accepted in spite of the Model A's reputation, thereby demonstrating that besides her freckled smile and good loaves, she also had spunk.

The combination of natural affinities, the isolation of our postings, and the assistance of well-intentioned community conniving—not to mention the moonlight—ought to have produced spectacular results. Alas, the advantage of our respective roles in the community, which up to this point had been more effective than a surveyor's transit in bringing us into close proximity, now turned against us in the form of inhibiting responsibility. The compass needle that ought to have pointed to true passion went haywire in the scrapyard of scruples. I marvelled at the power of Dr. Davey's prayer. His supplications on behalf of my boyhood innocence were still being answered.

Although Marjorie and I became close friends, the community was denied the pleasure of a full-blown romance that would have fed the chattering gossip mills for years to come.

Too soon the school year ended. Marjorie left and did not return in the fall. Pastoral visiting went into a slight decline around Smoky Burn, and I spent the rest of the summer, in fact the rest of my life, wondering every now and then about a road not taken.

Once the regular school year ended it was time to concentrate on arranging vacation Bible schools in each of the three communities. I couldn't imagine boys and girls recently freed for the summer showing much enthusiasm for an organized program that was to be held in the schoolhouse. I was wrong. For children from scattered frontier farms, vacation Bible school was infinitely more desirable than staying home to help with chores. They came by the truck load, dressed in their best patched clothing and hand-me-downs. Volunteers arranged for their delivery and pick up, although some walked a mile or more each way to be there. John McEwen usually came with his Shetland pony and trap, and the pony was tethered on the shady side of the schoolhouse, its tail swishing flies till its master was ready to go home.

Soon the schoolhouses resounded with excited squeals and lovely laughter as boys and girls from preschool to teenage years joined together in games and singsongs, crafts and stories, picnic lunches, and nature lessons. A team of "Caravaner" volunteers, aided by local teenagers—Sheila and Carol Parker in Battle Heights and Daisy Mae White in Smoky Burn—conducted most of the vacation Bible school activities. Selfishly, however, I reserved the storytelling period for myself.

At story time a squall of fidgeting gradually settled into rapt attention from the circle of upturned faces around me. Little mouths gaped and eyes widened as, in simple language, I told the wondrous stories found in the Old and New Testaments. Admittedly, I sometimes got carried away with my own recounting. I might act the part of David swinging his sling, then switch roles and fall Goliath-like on the dusty floor, claps and cheers of victory going up from the circle of listeners. I could be Moses striking the teacher's desk with a rod of alder to get water in the dusty desert, or Samson, armed with the jawbone of a moose, defeating a thousand Philistines coming through the front door, renamed "Ramath-lehi." On a patch of grass a little way from the school we fed the multitude, including John's pony and some red-winged blackbirds, by opening our lunches and sharing them. And you should have seen diminutive Gordie Rowan, his oversized cap coming down about his ears, passing out water converted to Freshie at the marriage feast of Cana—a miracle of love and imagination.

These were moments and hours that I treasured, for the children, many of them shy from isolation, their lives totally devoid of modern amenities, responded with such uncritical joy. They were easy to be with and it took very little to give them pleasure. Sometimes, at the end of the Bible school day, standing on the step of the schoolhouse watching them depart, a gentle wave of emotion passed over me, like a breeze bending tall grain. Excitedly they showed off their achievements in crafts to whomever came to pick them up, or they trudged with their trophies along the dusty road towards their homes. The plywood walls of many a kitchen and living room throughout this wild territory were decorated for years with gaudily painted plaster of Paris mouldings whose texts read, "God is Love," or "Jesus Loves Me"—proud creations and happy reminders of summer days at vacation Bible school.

The most obvious responsibility of the student minister was to conduct Sunday church services at each of the three communities. Papikwan presented its own challenges in this regard, but at Battle Heights and Smoky Burn people of many denominational backgrounds turned up to have their souls nourished on the lean liturgy of the United Church of Canada's plainest Order of Service.

In contrast to Christian liturgies that favour worship rich in ceremony built around the Mass or Eucharist, the streams of Protestant tradition that flowed into the United Church emphasize communication between God and humankind through "the written and spoken word." At the risk of over-simplifying, this means the Bible and preaching. A movement towards a more elaborate form of worship began working its way through the United Church from its inception in 1925, but at Battle Heights, Smoky Burn, and Papikwan we stuck with simplicity. The service was composed of the Call to Worship and Invocation followed by hymns of praise, prayers, and readings. Everything in the service moved inexorably towards the main intellectual and literary lump, the twenty-minute sermon, after which no one had energy for anything more than a closing hymn and the Benediction.

Presbyterianism—in which I had been raised and which, along with Methodism and Congregationalism, was one of the three main founding denominations of the United Church—put great stock in scholarship and preaching. I felt I should endeavour to uphold this tradition. I worked hard at the preparation and delivery of my sermons and even though the one-room schoolhouses were architecturally ill-suited to great oratory, this disadvantage was offset by the fact that I was in my early twenties, and therefore more certain of the truth than I would be ever again. I made the congregations full beneficiaries of this certainty. In turn, the people made gracious allowances for my youthful excesses, sifting the twenty-minute word avalanche for thoughts and ideas they could use and, often enough, finding ways to give me encouragement or guidance.

Gordon Rowan was one who urged me on in my preaching from the very first service in Battle Heights. It was a spring day and Gordon showed up early to light a fire in the woodstove to take the chill off the room. I also arrived well ahead of the eleven o'clock starting time so I could set up the portable pulpit and make sure everything was ready for the arrival of the worshippers. Gordon and I got chatting, which was fine, except that he kept absent-mindedly feeding chunks of wood into the stove till the fire was roaring up the chimney. Soon the room was like an oven. I was getting alarmed that the fire might even be out of control, but Gordon soon shut the damper and rubbed his hands with glee. "Well boy. I'll make it hot for them back here and you can make it hot for them up there," he chuckled.

Maintaining appropriate solemnity in the worship service wasn't always easy. There were distractions. One warm, summer day at Smoky Burn the schoolhouse desks were filled with children and farm folk. It was a good turnout. From the vantage point of the slightly raised platform upon which the teacher's desk supported the portable pulpit I looked over my congregation. A colourful collage of humanity it was. The women wore print dresses and laboriously ironed blouses, the men had sunburned faces glowing to the cap-line, and looked uncomfortably clean in their Vet's allowance suits. The children were uncommonly mud-free and had not yet started their customary shuffling and squirming. At the cost of providing free access to flies and mosquitos, the windows had been raised to create a merciful crossbreeze. The last vibrations of Rosemary Armstrong's ingenious efforts to draw music from the tuneless piano reverberated over the heads of the congregation and out across the schoolyard.

I rose to commence the service, conscious of my responsibility. The people had gathered. I was their minister, the servant of God through whose humble agency a Word of God might be heard by one of these souls. I delivered the words of the Call to Worship: "The Lord is in His holy temple. Let all the earth keep silence before Him."

"Bzzzz. Bzzzzzzz. Bzzz." A gigantic bluebottle frantically

banged its body against an upper window-pane, its altitude too high for the fly-through below. The amount of noise it made was astounding. I attempted to ignore it and continued with the Invocation.

"Let us pray."

"Smack." Harold Clisby had just obliterated a mosquito on his neck. He looked both relieved and embarrassed. I commenced the prayer of invocation.

"Almighty God, unto Whom all hearts be opened, all desires known, and from Whom no secrets are hid . . ." It remains a secret to this day which desk the next sound came from, but there was no mistaking the nature of it. The trumpet of the angel Gabriel could not have been more resounding. Or perhaps it was more like the blast from one of Joshua's trumpeters when the ancient walls of Jericho came tumbling down. The very amplitude of the report made it impossible to trace its origin but its effects were apparent almost immediately. There followed a wave of shuffling and frantic searches for handkerchiefs in purses and trouser pockets. Hymn books were deployed as fans. A plague of coughing broke out, and at the end of the prayer someone got up and added to the crossbreeze by opening the windows wider. The service didn't settle down again till well after the reading of the Gospel.

Smoky Burn was not alone in suffering disruptions to the mood of worship. At Battle Heights one Sunday, following the offering and announcements, just as the sermon was to begin, Charlie and Mary Parker's granddaughter Mary Lynne was playing with Mary's purse. Letting her have it seemed like a good way to keep her amused. Puzzling over the latch, the child wandered up towards the pulpit and out of Mary's reach, muttering something about how to open it. By now, people were struggling to control their amusement in an effort to uphold the dignity of the service. At the same time, anxiety was mounting as to what might happen next. They didn't have long to wait. I was announcing the text for the sermon when Mary Lynne discovered how to unlatch the purse. She peered into the deep recesses of the bag, then, with a piping voice that rose clearly above mine she exclaimed, "Oh Grandma, you didn't put all your pennies on the plate," whereupon she skipped the remainder of the way to the front and dumped the contents of Mary's purse onto the collection plate. Cash being scarce, I felt it was only right that Mary should be allowed to take change following the service.

The most calamitous event in a church service happened to none other than Charlie Parker. Charlie was a big man. To get himself into one of the school desks was an astounding accomplishment. How he managed to extricate himself for the hymns and at the end of the service was an even greater feat, though it must be said that, while there was obvious effort, he accomplished it with considerable gracefulness.

Charlie worked hard and he put in long hours. The year I lived with the family I often saw him so fatigued at the end of the day that he fell asleep on the step where he sat to take off his boots. As a frontier farmer he spent a lot of time moving about in the fresh air. It is not surprising, therefore, that the diminished oxygen supply and limited mobility during a church service in the schoolhouse taxed Charlie's capacity to stay awake. So did my sermons, apparently.

On this particular Sunday, no sooner had I commenced the sermon than Charlie's eyes took on a thick glaze, as usual. For a while he put up a valiant struggle to stay focused, but I could see he was losing it. His eyelids drooped. His chin sank onto his massive chest. Once or twice he jerked back from the edge of slumber, attempting to grasp meaning from the words that floated about him like butterflies on a summer day. Mary did her best to keep him awake with nudges, but recognizing defeat after a while, she limited her affectionate elbow-in-the-ribs treatment to moments when his snoring threatened to become tumultuous.

At the end of the sermon, following a short prayer, I announced the closing hymn and the congregation of about a dozen neighbours rose to sing. Charlie awoke with a start. Not wanting to be left behind he leapt to his feet, forgetting that there was a desk wrapped about his haunches. He and the desk went clattering across the floor in a series of grotesque leaps which, fortunately, left him and the desk in an upright position out in the aisle.

Assured that Charlie was not injured, we sang the hymn, I pronounced the Benediction, and we went home to dinner. Over dessert, Charlie told me he had found the sermon very interesting that morning.

CHAPTER 13

Gumbo

One morning in May of my second term as student minister, something happened that was to add a new dimension to my sojourn. I had resolved to visit some of the more church resistant residents of the Battle Heights area, and was on my way to do so when a movement in the ditch caught my eye. I jumped on the foot brake, geared down, drew back on the emergency and yelled, "Woooooh." As usual, the old Ford came to a sudden stop—some hundred yards further down the road. I threw the gearshift into reverse and shuddered back to the spot where I thought I had seen the movement.

On either side of the dike-like road were the ditches from which the road itself had been constructed. Throughout the territory these ditches were deep and often flowed like freshet streams, draining the saturated fields and forests, gurgling, mud-laden, down towards the river. By now, the worst of the spring run-off had been carried away so that the ditch, at least at this location, was a series of pools leaking one into the other at the bottom of a slope of mud.

I walked from the car along the lip of the ditch, scanning it's slimy sides and bed. It seemed empty, and I began to think that imagination had been playing tricks with my peripheral vision when a slight movement caught my eye. Gripped in the mud at the bottom of the ditch, its coat almost invisibly blended into the colour of the clay, was a tiny fawn.

As I came closer, it made a frantic effort to leap clear, but the mud was like quicksand. Its spindly legs plunged without effect till, exhausted, it lay gasping, with trickles of brown water swirling against its body. I hunkered down and stayed still, examining the tiny creature. It looked emaciated, and its flanks displayed every rib like fingers in a tight glove. It was smeared with clay, so that even the white spots on the back and sides were barely discernible. Mud clogged its snout and rimmed the great, desperate eyes. A slice of pink tongue hung from its mouth.

I had read *Lives of Game Animals*, by Ernest Thompson Seton, so I thought I had some knowledge about deer, though I had never actually seen one in the wild. To come upon this beautiful creature filled me with wonder. The initial emotion soured to sadness, however, and soon a strange feeling of indecency gripped me as I realized that I had blundered upon the scene of death, a drama at once private and sacred, yet commonplace out here where life and death abounded. This brief visitor to life was dying. Nature was snatching back what she had so recently given, and all the vast plains of pregnant fields, the greening groves of hardwood, and the forests laying seige to the scattered homesteads, were silent at the prospect. A scatter of clouds sailed carelessly across the sky in which the adolescent sun beat down with unpitying stare. Even the deserted road, empty as far as the eye could see, seemed to join with nature's mute chorus, pleading the necessity of indifference. The fawn lay very still save for the heaving of its sides. The world was still. I too, was still, watching, while pieces of recollected Seton locked into the jigsaw of my mind.

How the fawn had fallen into this deathtrap at the side of the road was a mystery, for Nature programmes into the scrawny four- or five-pound frame of a newborn white-tailed deer the instinct to stay put, and the doe will reinforce that instinct by applying pressure with her muzzle. The doe leaves her fawn ensconced in a thicket while she ambles off in search of food, for she needs a lot of nourishment to produce milk. By foraging far from the nursery and sneaking back for feedings, she avoids attracting attention to her young.

While the mother is gone, infant curiosity may drive the fawn to gambol a few yards from the thicket. These first excursions are dangerous. A coyote, or even a red fox that wouldn't dare tackle a nursing doe, would make a swift meal of an unprotected, milk-fed fawn. At the slightest sign of danger the fawn falls flat on the ground and remains perfectly still, the spotted coat blending into the forest floor like a splash of leaf-filtered sunlight, and since it has practically no body scent at this stage, the camouflage is usually effective. A person walking in the woods could almost step on a fawn before noticing it, or before it would move.

Somewhere in the distance a John Deere tractor started up, popping holes in the film of reverie that enveloped me. Now the ditch seemed to burst into a riot of industry with flies and insects speeding about their business. From the gnarled finger of a stricken spruce a quarter of a mile away, the mutter of a raven was carried on a current of air. It would wheel down and peck out the eyes of the victim in due time. The fawn struggled. Again it failed to extricate itself. If it was to thwart death, it would need help.

I knew enough to approach with caution, for the doe might not be far off and would resent any intrusion, no matter how well intentioned. A search of the surrounding area showed no mature hoof prints. As would be poignantly confirmed later that summer, deer frequently suffer accidents because of their haste when startled. Furthermore, the forests of this area were full of predators that would find an injured deer easy prey. Perhaps this is what had happened, and the fawn, despairing of its mother's return, had ventured from the thicket only to stumble into the ditch. I was never to know the answers to these questions. One thing seemed clear, however. Within an hour, perhaps less, this creature would be dead unless something was done.

One further thought occurred to me. After their first fawn, white-tails usually bear twins, even triplets, until their waning years. I walked along the bank till I found a spot where a chunk of timber had wedged into the mud, making it possible to get across. Then I searched the opposite bank and the field for several hundred feet in every direction, even crashing about in the tangle of briars and bushes where a bluff of woods abutted the field. There were no signs of the doe or other fawns. What I was going to do had to be a last resort for once the fawn was handled, if the doe was still alive, she would certainly forsake her offspring, so repugnant is the scent of humans to a deer's sensitive nostrils. However, there seemed to be no alternative. I started into the ditch.

Frightened by my approach, the fawn made another attempt to escape. Then it sank into the oozing muck, exhausted from the effort. For a moment I thought I had arrived too late. Besides, I was wondering what I was going to do if I did get it out alive. It was too young to fend for itself. Perhaps death was inevitable. Now, a day or two from now, what was the difference? As I slid down the bank, a muted bleating came from the fawn and it made another hopeless bid to leap free, its valiant will to live limited now by its ebbing strength.

It was not easy to reach the animal. I picked my way as cautiously as possible, using tufts of grass and occasional rocks and ridges of half-baked clay as stepping places, always edging towards the spot where the fawn lay panting. I was getting close when, somehow, I found myself straddling the bottom of the ditch, colossus-like, faced in the wrong direction. While planning a series of manoeuvres to get myself reorientated, my right foot disappeared into the quagmire, and the clump of sod upon which the left foot relied rapidly disintegrated. The limit of my limbs' elasticity was reached quickly, and I began to lose balance, which was preferable to what might have been lost had my feet continued sliding in opposite directions. Flapping my arms like a rooster on a shaky fence was of no avail. Down I went, making a last second, wrenching lunge towards the driest spot within range. One shoe was sucked off my foot and my body, while missing the absolute worst area, landed in the slime, my face coming to rest a foot from the head of the fawn. We looked at one another, both of us bewildered. The fawn remained silent. However, had anyone been within a half-mile radius of the scene they might have marvelled at the variety of mildly un-ministerial expletives emanating from the depths of the ditch.

From this point on there was little purpose in caution. I pulled the fawn into my arms and held it closely to keep its legs from thrashing. Its heart thumped rapidly against my hand. It was trembling. Climbing back out of the ditch carrying a shoe and a sporadically lurching armful of wild life was no easy feat. Twice we went sliding back down the bank, accumulating more layers of mud each time, but eventually I managed to crawl out with my living load, which I deposited in the back seat of the Model A.

The fawn turned out to be a reluctant passenger, which didn't surprise me. Most of my passengers were reluctant. The ride to my shack at Smoky Burn must have been terrifying for a fawn only a few days old. Showing remarkable powers of recuperation, it began battering the rear windows with its hoofs, till I was sure the glass would shatter. I had to stop a couple of times to wedge pieces of rag against the windows so they wouldn't slip open, and each time we got under way again the tattoo of miniature hoofs recommenced, mainly on the windows, but occasionally on the back of my head and shoulders, with near disastrous consequences for my driving.

The fawn fought all the way to Smoky Burn. The noise,

the confinement, the speed, and probably worst of all, the presence of a human, must have been abhorrent to this wild creature. I contemplated stopping to let it go, but I realized it would not survive on its own. The bush has no food for a motherless fawn that relies on milk for its first four to five weeks of life. Besides, just a few days earlier one of the farmers had shot a huge timber wolf prowling at the edge of a field of cattle. I went to view it and was amazed at its size. A fawn would not last long in the bush without the protection and cunning of its mother. I would have to be a surrogate mother for a while, and it would have to share my quarters till I figured out what to do next.

It was not impressed with my hospitality. As I carried it from the car through the sapling poplars towards the shack, it was fairly placid, but once inside, its terror was complete and the consequences were disastrous. When I took water and a cloth to wash the mud from its snout, and the "consequences" from the floor, it stepped on the edge of the basin and sent a wave of water across the linoleum. Then, as I tried to mop up the mess, the creature proceeded to skate and slide back and forth across the slippery surface. Its fine legs flashed in a tremendous burst of speed, but because there was no traction on the wet, hard surface, its body stayed relatively stationary till it crashed to the floor and went sliding across the room, coming to rest in an undignified position against the opposite wall.

Although my examination of the evidence was cursory, I deduced that the fawn was a male, and decided that he should have a name. Because he had been plucked from the mud, and since the basin was handy, I baptized him "Gumbo," my very first baptism.

I warmed some milk and placed it in a saucer before him but he promptly danced on it. Resignedly, I reached for the mop. After several unsuccessful attempts to get him to eat, I had the cleanest floor, the hungriest fawn and the most frayed set of nerves in the territory. Clearly, a different approach to feeding was required. I left Gumbo in the manse, hopped into the Model A, and rumbled off to the co-op store to pick up the supplies I figured would be needed.

The Smoky Burn Co-op was a simple frame building, not much larger than my shack. It offered staples such as tea, sugar, coffee, flour, rice, a few canned goods, light confectionary, and general conveniences. It had a sparser inventory by far than did Barney's place at Battle Heights. It was always on the brink of bankruptcy because there was very little cash in the community. The people lived mainly off the land. Indeed, had it not been for the post office franchise it would never have generated enough business to pay its managers the meagre salary they earned for their long hours and strenuous efforts, which included hauling mail and supplies from Carrot River in all kinds of weather. Bud and Louella Kowalsky, who had managed the store during my first year, had left the community. It was now run by Duff and Lorna Watts who lived with their young family in cramped quarters behind the store. The building sat on skids not far from the schoolhouse and the teacherage, its mud-splattered clapboard forming a conspicuous portion of the closest thing the community had to a visible centre.

It ought to have been a simple enough purchase, but Duff got this pained look on his face when I asked for a bottle of Coke and a baby-bottle nipple. For a moment he just froze in his tracks.

"A what?" he asked, more loudly than I thought necessary considering the presence of a pair of muddy farmers who were standing near the unlit stove, postponing their departure with pop and short gusts of conversation. "For a minute I thought you said a baby-bottle nipple," he laughed.

"Well, actually, I did," I retorted. "And a Coke, please," I added quickly, emphasizing the word, Coke. Duff hesitated before deciding to deal with the part of the order he was sure of.

"Opened?"

"No thanks," I replied, realizing that if I drank the Coke in the store I would have to leave the bottle behind. "I'll take it along with the—the other thing," I trailed off. Duff and I were about the same age and as the summer wore on we became good friends. Right now, he handed me the bottle of Coke, spread both hands on the counter, leaned confidentially toward me and, between fragments of a fractured laugh, verified again what he thought he had heard.

"You—you didn't say you wanted a—a nipple, did you?"

"Yep. You know—a baby-bottle nipple." I tried to sound casual, but I felt like a priest trying to buy a condom at a parish bake sale. My voice involuntarily grew husky and I had to clear my throat. "Hmm-mmm! The strongest kind you have," I added, feeling that if the order was shored up with specifications it might sound more plausible. Duff's eyes shot heavenward, showing a lot of white.

"Sure. Whatever you say. No problem. One, strong, baby-bottle nipple," he repeated between clenched, nicotine-stained teeth while stepping towards a display-card stapled with rows of nipples in individual cellophane wrappers hanging on the wall behind the counter. Around the cold stove an embargo on conversation seemed to be in force. Duff got close to the card of wrapped nipples, but before actually touching it, he looked over his shoulder towards me. A knowing smile suddenly flooded his face. Relieved, he sauntered back to where I was standing at the counter. Duff was nobody's fool. There was no way he was going to be taken in by a smart-ass college guy from back east. He fixed me firmly with one blue eye while the other squinted almost shut, his whole face screwing up to do it. "A baby-bottle nipple?" he articulated, the pitch of his voice rising about an octave higher than usual before spluttering into laughter. "I hafta admit, you almost got me," he chuckled.

"No, I'm not kidding, Duff. I really need one," I said, holding his gaze. "I'll explain later." We were into a stare down.

The silence behind me was oppressive. So much so that I contemplated telling Duff and the now unabashedly curious audience why I, a bachelor student minister, supposedly living alone in a shack on the corner of Bill and Peggy Kowalsky's farm, was buying a baby-bottle nipple along with a Coke. Truth is, I was afraid an explanation would create more difficulties than it would solve. I had an uncomfortable suspicion I might be breaking a law, or at the very least some folk conventions against raising wild animals in captivity. If I was, I didn't want to know about it.

However,the main reason I didn't mention the fawn was that in this territory, deer were not regarded with affection. They were a nuisance. The territory of Battle Heights, Smoky Burn, and Papikwan, lying between the southern edge of the forests and the northern extremities of the parklands, formed ideal deer country with its mixture of natural grassy glades, muskegs, and wooded groves. Burned-over and cut-over areas sprang up with tender poplar, willows, red-osier, chokecherry, and wild-rose and saskatoon bushes that made perfect feeding for deer. Here the fields of grain were like clearings in the bush. Deer could skulk out of the forest to feed on crops and with one bound disappear again.

Even though the winter of 1955-56 had been a hard one, the deer population in the region was up around thirty white-tails per square mile—ten times higher than the human population. No wonder these people wasted little sentiment on the beast. Deer were pests that trampled crops and chewed up gardens. In the fall they were food. I had no intention of telling anyone about Gumbo. At least, not yet.

Duff's stare faltered. I caught him shoot a furtive glance

past my shoulder as though he too was now conscious of the customers at the dead stove. He licked his lips, and for a moment I thought he was going to lose his composure completely, but he suddenly reached for the card of nipples and brought the whole display back to the counter, whereupon he began to extol the merits of the design, the texture of the rubber, the length, the grip on the bottle. I had never known him to take this much interest in his wares. Usually he swung back and forth between shelves and counter, plunking products onto the bleached wooden top, waiting wordlessly with poised pencil to jot down the next item on the bill while smoke from his dangling cigarette corkscrewed up into his eye, causing him to squint. When I asked how much I owed him, he shrugged.

"Don't worry about it right now," he said, reaching across the counter to pat me a friendly blow on the arm. "Who knows," he said, "you might decide you don't need it. If you do, why, just leave it in the wrapper and bring it back, o.k.?" I paid for the Coke and turned to go. Duff was shaking his head as I left and I had the impression that the place burst into conversation the moment the door shut behind me.

Back at the shack, Gumbo had busied himself with a thorough exploration of his surroundings, no doubt looking for any possibility of escape. In my haste to get to the store I had left the basin full of dirty water on a chair. It now lay upside down on the floor. A rod and reel with several hundred feet of fishing line, which usually stood against the cupboard behind the door, now lay in tangled spirals, ensnaring table and chairs and Gumbo himself. With a resigned sigh I waded across the floor and began unravelling him.

I knew the nipple would fit because I had noticed several of the women using pop bottles to feed their babies, so I guzzled the Coke and washed the bottle. Next, my mind turned to the Kowalsky goat. Without any knowledge of the matter, it seemed to me that goats might be more closely related than cows to the deer family. The goat and I were not on good terms, however, ever since I had retrieved a pair of jeans that I had washed and thrown over some saplings to dry. She had already devoured most of one leg by the time I arrived on the scene, resulting in an unusual tug-o-war, rendered difficult because the goat was more into charging and butting than pulling. In any event, our tenuous relationship notwithstanding, the goat was in one of her rare dry spells. Cow's milk would have to do.

A synthetic nipple on the end of a pop bottle bears little resemblance to the soft, white down on the underside of a nursing doe. However, Gumbo was hungry, so after I forced the thing into his mouth a few times and he got a taste of the honey-sweetened, warm milk, he sucked with such vigour that the nipple popped off the bottle. It didn't matter. I had to mop the floor again anyway, for the total trauma had not been good for the fawn's digestive system.

Sleeping arrangements proved to be even more difficult. With an armful of straw from the barn I made a bed beside some boxes in the corner and pressed Gumbo down onto it. But the moment I turned out the lamp to lie down on the rasping springs of the cot, he was up, thrashing about the cabin, knocking over everything movable. After several unsuccessful attempts to impress upon him the need for a good night's sleep, I constructed a corral using the boxes of clothes and junk. Into this enclosure I threw the straw and then, just as unceremoniously, Gumbo. The clatter of his hoofs on the boxes and walls kept up most of the night. Next day I conceded that the deer's nocturnal instincts were not going to adapt to the human habit of sleeping for up to eight hours at a time. I went back to the store and bought a small dog collar, this time telling Duff about the fawn. Throughout the day Gumbo was tethered to a sapling among the poplars outside the shack. At bedtime he was relegated to an empty granary while I slept.

Feedings with Gumbo became moments of great tenderness for me. While he braced himself on outstretched forelegs, rump high in the air, nuzzling and tugging at the substitute teat, which I learned to tie securely onto the bottle, I could admire the details of his beauty. White polka dots were flung in carefree lines down his back and sides. There was valiance in the sweep of his chest, gracefulness in the long sinewy neck, speed and strength in every fibre of his slender legs. The brow was darker than his beige cheeks, giving him an air of intelligence. The ears were alert antennae, cocking to sounds I could not hear, and his black button nose twitched to scents far beyond human range. The underside of his fluffy tail was snowy white—a flag to be flashed when in danger. White-tail! Above all, the infinitely dark eyes were beautiful beyond description. The mystery of being was in their depths.

I kept nursing Gumbo from whatever pop bottle was at hand, and the bond between us grew. I found myself anxiously racing home to be with him; to look into those deep, dark eyes; to feed him; and to stroke his silky coat while he nuzzled me with his snout and licked my ear for the taste of salt. Sometimes I lay down a few feet from him on the grass between the poplars, not moving, simply admiring him, being with him.

Following the advice of the game warden whom I had gone to see in Carrot River, I got rid of the tether soon after observing him nibble some leaves. It was the warden's opinion that if I did this he would be fully wild again by fall. However, for some time he seemed loathe to go far from me. At times he goaded me into playing games of hide and seek among the young poplars around the shack; he hid and I sought. He followed me to the woodpile when I went to fetch fuel for the stove. He even pursued me to church one Sunday, appearing like an apparition in the open doorway of the schoolhouse, then swiftly fleeing so that the only evidence of his having been there, as far as the congregation was concerned, was a slight, unaccountable halt in the reading of the lesson that day.

Gradually I saw less and less of him. For a while he showed up in the evenings for a feeding, approaching me ever more cautiously. When I weaned him completely he vanished, and for several weeks I saw no trace of him. Then, one evening as I was heading into the shack, he appeared from among the poplars. The first thing I saw was that he was already noticeably larger. Then, as he stepped forward my heart sank. He was limping, one hind leg dangling uselessly. How it had happened I would never know, but he had broken his leg. In his pain and distress he had come back to me.

The only way I could think of helping him was to put him swiftly out of his misery. I borrowed Bill Kowalsky's .22 rifle and a couple of shells. Like a faithful friend, Gumbo innocently followed me to the thickets beyond the yard. When I halted he stopped. Reluctantly, I raised the gun and pointed it at the centre of his head, my finger on the trigger. He stood still, his enormous, soft eyes looking directly into my soul, ignorant of the lethal weapon aimed at his brain. In the moment I hesitated he limped to my side, stretched up, and licked my ear. A choking lump expanded in my throat. Methodically, I unloaded the rifle and laid it on the ground. I put my arm around Gumbo's neck and patted him. Something warm and wet brushed my cheek. It was Gumbo's tongue licking away a tear.

I couldn't follow through with what I had thought necessary, but an alternative began to take shape in my mind. Somehow I managed to get him into one of the granaries in which there was a small pile of wheat. At the co-op store I bought several rolls of gauze bandage. I let myself into the school, rummaged through a box of supplies used for crafts at vacation Bible school and found what I was looking for—a couple of tongue depressors and a brown paper bag of plaster of Paris powder. Back at the shack I picked up the basin and some water.

Gumbo wouldn't lie down for me, but by standing him in the pile of grain, stroking him, talking softly and allowing him to lick my ear, I was able to get the ends of bone lined up and to apply a pair of tongue depressors as splints, wrapping them, not too tightly, with the bandages that I ran through the plaster of Paris mixed in the basin. It was no work of art, and I had almost as much plaster on myself as I did on Gumbo, but the paste hardened swiftly and when I had finished the leg was firm and he limped without putting that hoof to the ground.

A fawn with a cumbersome plaster cast! I couldn't let him run free. So, once again he was tethered to a sapling close to the shack and sometimes I supplemented his diet of leaves and shoots with treats of porridge and milk. However, this didn't last long, for one evening, after less than a week, I came home to find he was gone, the dog leash and rope still tied to the sapling. Not wanting to make the lease too tight around his neck I had been too generous in the size of the loop and he had managed to slip his head out of it.

Desperately, I scouted the surrounding bluffs and thickets. I saw tracks from time to time, small hoof marks, sometimes droppings, but I couldn't find him. I searched as often as possible, but even though I was worried that the cast would make him easy prey for predators, I was busy with my duties, frequently not getting back to the shack till late in the evening.

The weeks passed. A new sharpness laced the evening air. Harvesting began, and it was time for me to head back east to resume my studies. The evening before leaving Smoky Burn I went for a walk behind Kowalsky's farm, further than I had gone before, past the sapling poplars, deeper into the woods. I held little hope of seeing Gumbo, but I had to make one last search.

Following a narrow trail I moved slowly and quietly, scanning the ground for tracks, watching through the trees for any sign of movement. Nothing! Daylight was fading and an eerie stillness I hadn't noticed before gripped the forest. My mind told me there were no animals in the woods that I needed to fear, not even the bears that sometimes came out to maraud around the livestock, nor the timber wolves I often heard howling at night. I stopped. Everything was deathly quiet.

Since there was nothing to be afraid of, I decided to turn around and get out of there as quickly as possible. I had gone only a short distance when an explosion of muscle and sinew erupted from a thicket a few yards off the trail. A ferocious bear—no; a ravenous wolf—no; a young deer, thank God, its white tail flagging, sprang into flight, bounding gracefully over a fallen log, zig-zagging through the trees in a series of powerful leaps. As it fled I caught a glimpse of what appeared to be a narrow white band on its left leg.

"Gumbo," I called out. "Gumbo. It's me. Here Gumbo." The young deer stopped. It looked back, nervously. I spoke to it softly. "Here Gumbo—o.k. boy—it's all right—come and see me." I stayed perfectly still, speaking softly as, step by step, ever so cautiously, the deer approached. I was upwind from him and I knew he would have picked up my scent. He kept coming, this fine looking young deer. His spots were almost completely gone now, and he showed hardly the trace of a limp as he walked, alert, looking as though he might leap into flight again at any moment. Twenty feet from me, he halted as though he would come no further, but in a moment he closed the remaining distance, came right up to me and licked my ear.

I patted his neck, but he startled, pulling his head back.

Without any swift movements I examined the leg that had been broken. A small, frayed portion of plaster cast remained. He had obviously chewed or rubbed most of it off. I thought if I could get him to come with me to the shack I would remove the remaining piece of plaster with scissors. He was too big now, and too wild, to attempt to carry or hold. The only way would be to keep talking gently to him and see if he would follow me. Slowly, I began walking along the trail, stopping every few yards to encourage him to follow. He did take a few tentative steps, but as we got closer to the edge of the forest he halted well back, and no amount of coaxing would entice him to take another step. I decided that perhaps I could simply pick the rest of the cast off, perhaps find an end of the bandage and unravel what remained. Still speaking in low, gentle tones, I cautiously moved towards him. Instantly, he was gone. The last I saw of Gumbo was the flash of his tail as he disappeared between the trees.

He was beautiful.

CHAPTER 14

Impenetrable Papikwan

Upon reflection spread over the better part of a lifetime, I believe I can say with confidence that my efforts to spread the Gospel and to extend the embrace of the Church in that district of northern Saskatchewan known as Papikwan, did very little harm. The main reason for this was that no one came to church services, where they might have been affected by my preaching, one way or the other.

Over the span of two summers, from April till September each year, in spite of home visiting and barrages of personal invitations to come to church, I cannot recall, apart from one notable exception, a bona fide service of worship complete with worshippers being held at Papikwan. At Battle Heights there was a faithful corps of church-goers who could be counted upon to show up even when it required slogging through mud to get there. At Smoky Burn there was a palpable sense of effort at building a community, and church was seen by a majority of the folk, even those who took religion with the proverbial "pinch of salt," as an integral part of community structure and a link with history and tradition. But at Papikwan, on Sundays when roads and weather permitted me to get there myself, I waited for worshippers at the schoolhouse door, week after week, like a forlorn storekeeper hoping for customers who never came.

In fairness, it has to be acknowledged that for anyone so inclined, church attendance would have been a difficult proposition. An extension of the Saskatchewan government's scheme to settle veterans on the land through co-operative farming, Papikwan was younger than Smoky Burn, and less "opened up." It was June 1950 before a government camp was set up not far from where The Pas trail crossed the Papikwan river, a tributary of the Carrot. Clearing was slower here because, although the area had been logged for its best spruce timber, heavy stands of white and black poplar remained along with some spruce groves, untouched by the forest fires that had "prepped" the land for clearing at Smoky Burn. Consequently, by the time Willowdale, Pleasant Acres, Papikwan, and Woodland co-operative farms were established, it was already into the fifties.

From all accounts, an enthusiastic spirit had prevailed in the initial days of Papikwan. The camp along the banks of the stream from which the district got its name was like a small village of rough-sawn lumber. There was the bunkhouse and a mess hall for bachelors. For married couples and their young families, as at Smoky Burn, the inimitable eighteen-by-twenty-four foot frame houses were built on skids so they could be hauled onto the farms once sufficient land was cleared. There was a conglomeration of workshops and sheds and even a tiny store owned by Maurice Greenberg where, although it wasn't really a post office, mail could be picked up provided a truck had been able to get into Carrot River and back that week.

To combat the isolation and deprivations of the frontier, the women of the camp formed The Jolly Club. Just how jolly the meetings turned out to be was a matter of imaginative speculation among the men folk, not to mention women of neighbouring districts, so that the club gained an alluring reputation. It was said, for example, that among the recipes exchanged by the women was one for a trenchant country wine that had to be—and often was—tasted to be believed. No doubt, some of the stories about The Jolly Club were exaggerated. In any event, the moral tenor of the nascent community seemed balanced, for earlier student ministers often managed to hold church services at the camp, with real people in attendance.

Before much settlement could be achieved, the project ran into the wet years and the early dreams soon became nightmares of hardship. Machinery got bogged down. Land clearing and breaking proceeded at a torturously slow pace or came to a complete halt. On the little land that was broken and cultivated crops could not be planted because of the rain, or if they were planted, could not be harvested because the land was too wet.

By the mid-fifties, when I was there, the co-operative farms had failed, and a majority of the initial settlers had left the territory, either permanently or to find paying jobs, hoping to return under more favourable conditions. Those who remained to farm individually were practically destitute and were driven by the demands of daily survival. Sunday or not, if the land was dry enough to get machinery onto it the men would be working.

For the women, wrestling with small families in shacks devoid of conveniences, life was equally hard. Several of the women I visited told me they would like to come to church. If nothing else, it would be a welcome reprieve from the relentless cycle of chores, but endless toil held them hostage.

To add to the difficulties, the roads around Papikwan were abominable. The Pas logging trail was still the principal connecting link with Carrot River, while the track running north to Smoky Burn traversed the bog and was frequently impassable even when other roads were dry. Many Sundays neither minister nor congregation could have been faulted for not getting to church due to inclement weather and poor road conditions.

On those Sundays, once I realized the roads were impassable, I would settle down to enjoy an afternoon of reading, or perhaps have a snooze in preparation for the possibility of an evening service at Smoky Burn or Battle Heights, roads and weather permitting. Although a candidate for the ministry of The United Church, I had been raised Presbyterian, and therefore, naturally, could not expect to indulge in such unabashed leisure without paying a penalty of guilt for indolence. On the other hand, Presbyterianism had its compensations, because failure to deliver my sermon to a full schoolhouse could always be written off against "predestination," something like a non-refundable sin credit. These two fundamentals of Calvinistic Protestantism frequently marred an otherwise pleasurable Sunday afternoon by squawking over my soul like a pair of bluejays teasing a cat. Generally, just before dozing off, I would have it reasoned that since God was responsible for the weather, He (none of us was in any uncertainty about the gender of God in those days) could hardly get into a divine huff over nobody being at the school to worship His Holy Name, considering He had dumped enough rain on the territory to refill Lake Agassiz. Then again, if He was not actually in direct control of the weather, we were all wasting our time going to church anyway, for—as in farm communities around the world—the main thrust of the prayers had to do with weather, either for rain or for the rain to stop. In northern Saskatchewan in the mid-fifties, all humble beseeching was for the rain to stop.

Often enough, my sense of responsibility (guilt dressed in a business suit), or heroism (guilt in the uniform of "aide-de-camp"), would motivate me to load the Model A with the collection plates and the other symbols of United Churchism, and in defiance of a deep-seated certainty that none of the settlers would be stupid enough to venture onto the roads, I would attempt to "get through." The response of the community to this demonstration of devotion to duty was touching. Those whose farms were situated where they could see the road and who, therefore, had a view of me grinding the transmission out of the Model A, would generally exclaim, "There goes that damn-fool student minister again." Later, one of them would crank up his tractor and come to pull me out of the mud.

I have to admit that I was disappointed when nobody showed up on the Sundays when I had rehearsed the sermon to my cracked mirror, put forth the effort to get there, and set up the clutter of religious paraphernalia that converted the school into "The House of The Lord." I would be displeased. Actually, I would be "pissed off," but being a student minister, I had to be content with being displeased.

When the roads were dry, and still there was no congregation, I often felt thoroughly discouraged. For without detracting from my own devotion to God at that time, nor the sincerity of any other cleric for that matter, and bearing in mind the mountain of theological argument in support of the efficacy of public worship, it must be recognized that at the heart of every church service is the tender ego of the preacher. I don't mind admitting that I was often downhearted when no one came to church at Papikwan.

Imagine my joy, therefore, when one hot Sunday, my persistence, my diligence in visiting and my determination in navigating the roads even to the point of foolhardiness, all finally seemed to be paying off. It was within minutes of the three o'clock starting time. I was sitting on the front steps of the schoolhouse absorbing the bone comforting heat of the sun, waiting for nobody to show up and preparing my spirits for the customary disappointment by watching a scurry of ants and listening to a symphony of flies and insects. It was amazing how loud they were. They filled the drowsy day with busyness. One fly in particular seemed to be unnaturally resonant, and it was getting louder. Or was it a bee, or a wasp? It had a different quality of sound, a hard kernel of noise folded into the softer background buzz. I suddenly realized that what I was hearing was not an insect at all. It was the sound of a vehicle. A grove of poplars skirting the schoolyard obscured my view, so I dashed to the road and looked away to the west where the sound seemed to be coming from, and there, sure enough, trundling along the trail and bearing down towards the school was a three-ton stake truck. What was encouraging was that, as far as I could tell, it was filled with people standing in the back, holding onto the stake sides.

I ran into the school to check that everything was in place: the Bible on the lectern with slips of paper marking the readings so it would look like I knew exactly where to find the texts; the order of service where I could refer to it easily; my sermon ready for dynamic delivery in due time, and securely tucked under a corner of the Bible where it wouldn't get blown away by an untoward breeze from the open windows; a hymn book on each desk; the gaping collection plates at the ready on either side of the cross. Everything was set. Back to the door I dashed in preparation for welcoming the worshippers. The truck was close now. I thought it was going a little fast for a comfortable swing into the schoolyard. With all those people standing in the back, the driver ought to be careful about suddenly applying the brakes. Still, I figured he knew what he was doing.

The truck shot into sight from behind the screen of poplars. Sure enough, it was loaded with people, men and women and youngsters all packed in together, bracing themselves against the lurching of the platform upon which they stood. As the vehicle came abreast of the school the driver did not apply the brakes. The only thing he applied was the horn, a long, mocking, cracked-voice goose-honk as the truck lumbered past the schoolyard, the passengers cheering and waving before being obliterated by the pursuing cloud of dust. They were off to play baseball.

I sat down on the steps, "disappointed." Gradually the diminuendo of the distancing truck was overlayered by the gentle cello sounds of the insects. A great fatigue gathered up my shattered spirits and held them together in the only vessel within immediate reach: indifference. I leaned back against the wall of the school and shut my eyes, resolving to wait another fifteen minutes, but hoping deep down that no one would come. A grasshopper ripped a kettledrum roll across the vibrato of the other insects. From a willow beside the ditch a red-winged blackbird badly botched a soprano aria.

Whether it was the bird or the grasshopper, I'm not sure, but suddenly, as though by divine revelation, I knew what had to be done. I sprang out of my lethargy and went into the school where I found pencil and paper and wrote a notice that I stuck on the rusted head of a nail beside the door. Then I gathered up the various pieces of church, shut the windows, locked the school, cranked the Ford, and headed off. The sign beside the door read: "Church at Ball Field Today."

Having been raised in Northern Ireland, I had never learned to play baseball. Like most lads in Ulster, I grew up with a soccer ball at my toe, and indeed, shortly after coming to Canada I signed on with London City in the Western Ontario Soccer League. In high school I made the senior rugger team in my first year, and was called to dress a few times for the village cricket team in Dunmurry. I knew very little about baseball, hardball, softball—whatever it was—but was confident that there couldn't be much to it for a reason-ably athletic fellow like myself. It looked like what we called "rounders" back in Ireland, and that was more or less a girls' game. I was determined to play ball. I would whack that ball right out of sight—in the Name of The Lord, of course.

The Model A clattered into the makeshift ball field just as sides were forming. I was brash with righteous resentment. "Hi," I greeted. "Since nobody showed up for church I figured

I might as well join you guys for a game of ball. Which side am I on?" There was muttering, a bit of banter and some rear-ranging. I believe one fellow was sent off the field to make room for me, but I didn't care. I was going to take out my frus-trations one way or another. I was told to go out to right field, which I did, in so far as I knew where that was. As long as the guy who was acting like captain waved me further out, I kept backing up, till I was beside the dense grove of black spruce that flanked the field, where all the mosquitos were. I knew immediately I was going to be busy, whether or not the ball ever came my way.

It didn't come my way for a long time. Indeed, everything in the game seemed to be happening somewhere else, and I found it quite lonely away out there beside the woods by myself, flailing at mosquitos. It was hard to maintain interest. "This is slower than cricket," I thought, and to while away the time I permitted my mind to wander, just a little. I can't remember what I was musing about, but I definitely was not concentrating on the game when a frantic yell went up from my teammates and the knot of mostly women and children spectators. The surge of noise caused me to look up just in time to see what appeared to be a meteorite falling out of the sky. Out of the corner of my eye I could see a heavy set fellow thundering around the bases in rubber boots. The ball had reached its apogee and was descending towards me at a speed that was in direct ratio to the rate at which mosquitos were plunging their proboscises into my ears and neck. The situa-tion called for swift decision making. Did I have time to swat once more or not? It was a choice between pain and pride. At great expense to my ear lobes I threw up my gloveless hands and went into an undignified dance to get under the ball, which seemed to be taking a last-minute swerve.

The meteorite smacked the heels of my hands and bounced back into the air. I made a fumbling grab that must have looked like I had resumed mosquito swatting. I was juggling the ball but couldn't hold it. A futile swipe knocked it sideways. With a sinking feeling I could see it out there, as though suspended for a split second, then falling, falling to the ground, just out of reach. With a desperate lunge I dove, arms outstretched, and to my own surprise, I felt my burning palms closing around the thing just as I hit the dirt. A roar of delirious approval went up from the stands as I held the ball aloft.

The truth is, there was no roar. There were no bleachers, no stands. There was a cluster of raggedly dressed pioneers, watching while their friends, their husbands, and fathers, outfitted in jeans and overalls and heavy boots, played softball on a Sunday afternoon with three mitts between both teams. There was no roar. There was, I believe, a slight, anxious gasp, then an outbreak of relieved laughter as the student minister with stinging hands and swollen ears threw the ball to second, having learned his most unforgettable lesson in baseball: that a softball is not soft at all.

The other thing I learned that day was that for all their lack of uniforms and equipment, these people were good ball players. As might be expected, they were mighty sluggers when up to bat. They were also smart fielders, swift and accurate throwers, and as I discovered to my dismay, the underhand pitching was cunning and lightening fast. I managed to connect with the ball only once in several turns at bat, and that flier was caught easily. My need to smash the ball into the woods went unsatisfied and my college-athlete ego was properly humbled, one ungainly catch failing to rank as an outstanding play.

I didn't even get to meet many of the people, for I spent most of the time beside the woods with the mosquitos. Yet, as I looked around at the faces of the players and spectators, I felt glad that these hard-working pioneers had taken time to play a game of softball on a Sunday afternoon. In a strange way, I suspected that the sign on the schoolhouse had turned out to be more prophetic than intended. Church had been at the ball field today. The people had congregated. There was a form of communion between them. Who was to say that God was not in their midst?

As I cranked the Model A and prepared to leave at the end of the game, I looked back at the motley group of people climbing into the rear of the truck. One or two of them waved and I waved back. Then, just before stepping into the car, I hesitated. Silently, I pronounced the Benediction. "The Lord bless you and keep you . . .," I thought. Then I drove off.

My participation in the game that day had no perceptible impact upon subsequent church attendance. The established trend continued unabated. Sunday after Sunday, the people of Papikwan denied themselves the unspeakable joys of the United Church Order of Service, not to mention the rivetting, pre-theology oratory that lay in wait for them at the one-room schoolhouse on the southeast quarter of 2-50-9-W2.

I countered this dearth of zeal for organized religion by briefly embracing a tradition in Church dogma which asserts that the service of worship is efficacious in its own right, whether or not the faithful are gathered at the altar. Admittedly, the roots of my own faith were too much embedded in the fissures of Reformation rock to sustain for long such luxuriant belief. However, following a run of empty Sundays at the Papikwan schoolhouse, the concept held powerful appeal, and I subscribed to the idea just long enough to conduct one service in which I preached a sizzling sermon directed at the empty desks, chiding them for their vacancy and upbraiding them for their emptiness.

One Sunday, however, there really was a congregation and the service was duly conducted. It was a service I would never forget. It was a brilliant, northern day, and I was enjoying the familiar strains of the insect orchestra on the schoolhouse steps when I was startled by the appearance of a woman emerging from the brush that camouflaged the trail. On her feet were cut-off rubber boots into which her rolled-down stockings drooped. The washed-out print dress she wore, with lopsided hem, may once have been predominantly blue. It was difficult to tell. Over it she wore a man's brown cardigan with tattered elbows, the sleeves turned up at the wrists. She clutched a bundle at her left shoulder, obviously a tiny infant. Flopping along in oversized rubber boots, sometimes skipping ahead, sometimes falling behind, was a little girl of three or four years of age. Her sister, also planted in rubber boots, acted old beyond her five or six years, as she herded the younger one like a patient sheepdog, keeping her away from serious harm, mainly the water-filled ditch. Both girls wore frilly dresses which, while they didn't fit, were newly washed and ironed.

I jumped up and walked swiftly to the road to meet them. I didn't recognize them. "Hi," I greeted. "I'm Hugh McKervill. I'm the student minister. Nice to see you." Inwardly I admonished myself. "Who else would she think you were, dummy, an Encyclopedia Britannica salesman?"

"Hi," said the woman, smiling broadly but averting her eyes out of shyness. I think she must have given me her name and the names of the children, but I failed to make a written note and they have long ago been lost to memory.

"Hello. How are you today?" I said, turning to the girls. The younger one responded by flinging her arms around her mother's leg and pressing her cheek against the fleshy security. The mother almost stumbled as she unbuckled the arms with one hand while clinging to the baby with the other. The older girl scowled, rolled her eyes up into her long-suffering little head and tugged her sister free from the leg. "Have you walked far?" I asked.

"Not too far. A couple of miles, I guess," the woman replied. There was perspiration on her brow.

"You must be tired. Here, would you let me carry the baby?"

"Sure," she chuckled, and handed me the bundle.

Together we walked towards the school and went in.

We all clumped to the front of the room and the mother squeezed her abundant body into the desk to the left of the improvised communion table and pulpit. The smaller girl hung close to her mother. The older sister took her position in an adjacent front desk and immediately began paging through the hymn book in a futile search for pictures. For a while, the woman and I chatted about the rain, the roads, the crops, the possibility of more people arriving for the church service, anything we could think of, till it was painfully clear that there would be no more worshippers. Finally I said, "It doesn't look like anyone else is going to join us. Are you comfortable with me going ahead with the service?" She was a big woman, with round ruddy cheeks and she was having difficulty cooling off after the long walk.

"Oh yes. We might as well go ahead," she said, fanning her flushed face with the hymn book. "I don't get to church very often," she added wistfully. I handed her back the baby and went to the pulpit.

Church services are relatively formal affairs, the degree of formality being largely, though not entirely, dependent upon the denomination. By design, human intimacy is discouraged. The very arrangement of furniture and ceremony precludes it. For example, the minister is ensconced in a fortress-like pulpit, usually raised above the congregation and set a nice distance away from the people who sit in obedient rows with little or no opportunity for communication between them. Even when there is conversation, usually before the service begins, it is always in subdued whispers. This is all for good liturgical reasons, but somehow, the normal United Church Service, as I knew it, seemed ill-suited to a congregation comprised of one adult, two restless little girls, and a sleeping baby, all sitting just a few feet from the minister. On the other hand, when I thought of the effort this woman had made to come to church with her children, I felt she deserved a proper church service. I decided to stick to the Order of Service but to avoid the lofty, "objective" approach.

Things went along nicely for a while. I moved away from the protection of the pulpit from time to time, sometimes sitting on the teacher's chair to be on the same level and to explain different elements of the service. Then I moved back to the pulpit to add import to parts of the service such as The Reading of The Word, or The Prayers of Intercession. I sang the hymns for them, inviting them to join in if they felt like it. The mother followed the words in the hymnal and the girls stared in utter amazement. It didn't seem appropriate to deliver a sermon in the usual way, so I sat down again and chatted about the text and ideas I had intended preaching. I even managed to get the attention of the girls for a while by telling the story of the five loaves and two fishes in my own words. This worked well until something more urgent intervened.

The smaller girl had been getting more and more restless, squirming and writhing about her mother's desk. A couple of times she had attempted to whisper in her mother's ear but she was gently pushed away, the woman not wishing to offend me by dividing her attention. But, shortly after one of these rebuffs the child piped up urgently, "Mummy I gotta pee." This definitely got attention and the older girl promptly escorted her sister to the outhouse.

By now, the baby, who had been a model of tranquillity, started to fuss. What started as a whimper rapidly moved through squirming and squawking to crying and then full blown screams of rage. It was astounding how such a tiny creature could make so much noise. I was drowned out. The mother was growing more and more disconcerted. The poor soul tried gallantly to maintain interest in what I was saying while rocking, shushing, patting, or bouncing the baby in unsuccessful attempts to restore peace and order. All her efforts were in vain. The service was coming apart. I gave up attempting to speak and was looking on helplessly, wearing a benign smile of sympathy, when the mother deftly opened her dress, took the huge, bulbous breast that fell out in her hand and shoved it into the baby's mouth.

The silence was immediate. So was my embarrassment. Being in my early twenties, from a conservative, Anglo-celtic background, I did the only thing that occurred to me. I kept on preaching, except that now I began discovering chinks in the ceiling that I had never noticed before.

After the service I offered to give them a drive, but the woman told me that not far from the school the trail was impassable and that I would only get stuck. I walked to the road with them, the smaller girl holding my hand as we went. At the road I bid them good bye. "Bye-bye girls. I hope I'll see you again soon." They were already skipping away. I turned to the mother. "God Bless," I said as I shook her partially free hand.

"Thank you reverend," she said. "It was a lovely service."

She turned and trudged along the trail.

CHAPTER 15

Harvest Home

Too soon the summer ended, and as the air was honed to a new sharpness, so too, a disquieting current of mixed emotions disturbed the inner weather of my being. I had graduated from Waterloo in the spring and was now looking forward to commencing theological studies at Emmanuel College, University of Toronto. I was excited by the prospect of finally comprehending what the Reverend Gordon Toombs had been talking about back when I first arrived in Carrot River. It was about as exciting as theological studies would ever get, as it turned out. At the same time, I felt regret at the thought of leaving Battle Heights, Smoky Burn, and Papikwan, for during my second term as student minister, something unforseen had happened. I had become attached.

Paradoxically, the natural environment that, for much of the time I was there, had been a cheerless mess of mud and murderous mosquitos, had ultimately beguiled me with its harsh beauty. Even breathing the northern air was a sensuous pleasure. Tinctured as it was with spruce, and laced with the mouldy bouquet of tilled earth, an early morning draught of it could intoxicate the spirit for the day ahead. For someone who had grown up in hilly country and in cities, the most compelling aspect of nature was not the flat land. It was the panoply of boundless sky above the land. Flawlessly blue, or filled with argosies of urgent cloud, its kaleidoscopic features carried hope of bounty or the threat of failure to those who tilled the earth.

Bordering the frontier of cultivation, stood the presentient forest, full of stealthy life, with wary ravens circling reconnaissance along its dark fringes. As the forest receded before the breaking plough, daylight danced between the windrows and across the broad fields spreading out to shimmering horizons. Their hues changed with the seasons—from winter white to seed-time black, gossamer green of spring deepening to verdant summer, flax blue alternating with rapeseed yellow followed by the sturdy golds of autumn. The days were a riot of colour. At the close of day the northern horizon glowed from the ember of the sun shallowly dipped beneath its surface, and the gem-strewn heavens became a cosmic screen upon which danced the phantasmagoric Aurora Borealis.

I would miss all this. Here, at the edge of human habitation, nature was expansive, intense, demanding. She challenged the mettle of people. Those who endured her capricious ways while trying to shape and harness her energy to bring forth food, developed not only calloused hands and sunburned necks. They developed character. Soul without sanctimony. As I prepared to leave, I knew that it was a good place for a student of the soul to have spent some time.

As the day for my departure grew closer I also realized how much I would miss the abundant animal life, both wild and domestic. Shortly before leaving I paid a last visit to the Parkers in Battle Heights. Naturally, the chickens put on a neurotic display of nervous disquiet as I wheeled into the yard with the Model A. I ignored them, however, and sneaked into the barn to see the Guernsey cow. She swung her ponderous head around to look at me as I stepped into the dusky stillness. Strange, how I was so fond of her. Over time, I had even discovered a friendliness in the smell of manure, which I now savoured and bottled in memory. After a while I reached out and patted the Guernsey's face and said goodbye. She stopped chewing, and for a long moment she gazed at me with her big, watery eyes, before resuming her resolute munching. Could it be that something of my essential self had connected with whatever it was that made her a living being? I wondered. Certainly, when you stop to think about it, an almost unique level of intimacy had been established between us. Even in the realm of human relationships, over the span of a normal lifetime, you don't put your face up against the warm belly of very many people.

Besides farm animals there was the profusion of wild life: from mice and moles in the fields, to beaver, minx, martin, and weasels along the banks of the Carrot river. There were deer, elk, and moose, as well as foxes, coyotes, red squirrels, timber wolves, and black bears in the bush, often enough right in the farmyards. There were pickerel and northern pike to be pulled from the cloudy waters of the river, and the air was busy with a plethora of bird species ranging from hummingbirds to bald eagles. Prairie chickens and ruffed grouse were abundant. Canada geese heading south in the fall often stopped to feed on grain, and during these wet years flocks of mallard ducks would swim in the flooded fields eating the tops off the wheat.

Menacing though certain species were, without the plentiful wildlife it is doubtful anyone could have survived, either during the early, broadaxe days of pioneering around Battle Heights, or in the mechanized, post-war push to open up the land in all three districts. Wild game provided money-fetching fur as well as meat for food. On some of the farms there were children approaching their teens who had never tasted ordinary beef.

Quite beyond such practicalities, however, it seemed to me that the tone of human existence was affected by the presence of so much wildlife. Even the spine-chilling howls of coyotes and timber wolves in the night were a reminder that the darkness beyond the lick of yellow lamp light was not void, that there was abundant life extraneous to the human domain. We are not alone in this world. Whether it was a steer following my footsteps in the night, the sense of peace I found in the barn with the Guernsey cow, the comically assertive personality of the Kowalsky goat, or the love and care I had experienced for a tiny fawn, I ended the summer convinced for ever that the gap between animal beings and being human is not nearly as great as our civilization has made it out to be.

I was pleased that I had returned for a second summer. The experience had taken me a step beyond "spectatorship" to a more intimate connection with the land and its creatures. I had also deepened my bond with the people. Real Canadians they were, who worked so terribly hard to earn a living and to make a place for themselves and their children, and who, in so doing, were unself-consciously building a nation. Only during my second year did I begin to fully comprehend the heroic human history I had been witnessing, and in some minuscule measure, had been privileged to be a part of.

There was no mistaking the serious sense of grim determination that hung over the communities during the years I was their student minister. The wet years, which lasted from 1949 through to 1957, had taken their toll. Yet in spite of this, there was a lot of good-natured joking, strong friendship, and community fun.

Pleasure came in unsophisticated packages. Maybe a spontaneous ball game would be organized, or a group of women and children would get together to pick raspberries, saskatoon berries, high-bush cranberries, pin cherries, or blueberries. Visiting in each other's homes for a game of cards and a treat of homemade cake was common.

The big event of the year at each of the communities was Sports Day. Children and adults joined in the many races and relays. At Smoky Burn, Duff Watts and I squared off for a one-mile run on the baked road, the course ending beside the co-op store where we could immediately quench the ensuing thirst with pop. We were pretty well matched and came in neck and neck with an impressive hundred-yard sprint. Duff was the better runner, however, for I had canvas shoes. He ran in heavy leather boots.

At the core of Sports Day were the men's and women's ball games played against neighbouring communities. I played ball a couple of times in make-up games, but on Sports Day, community honour was at stake, so I was diplomatically left off the team. I seem to recall being offered to a visiting team, but they had seen me play before and graciously declined my services.

When the ball game ended people went home for a while, for there were chores to do. Later in the evening the activities resumed with a dance in the schoolhouse, and if some of Mary Little's dandelion wine, or a bottle of Parker's "Eight-Eighty-Eight" was on the go, as it usually was, spirits could rise to dizzying heights.

The last social event I attended was a joint community farewell held in the Smoky Burn schoolhouse to bid me goodbye. That my impending departure should occasion such widespread celebration was a bit disconcerting. Nevertheless, it turned out to be a time of music and speeches, of story telling, laughter, and fun. In emphasizing the contribution I had made to the level of religious understanding in the community, someone attested, "Why, we didn't know what sin was till you got here." In reply I scribbled a multi-versed ditty and sang it to the strum of my ukulele. Only three verses remain in memory:

> The river, it was flowing high,
> The roadways, they were never dry,
> And mud was splashing in my eye,
> On my first mission field.

I visit ladies by the score,
I come a-knocking at their door,
I wish that I could visit more,
On my first mission field.

My sermons, they are short and sweet,
The hymns we sing have all got beat.
Why do the people fall asleep,
On my first mission field?

The schoolhouse reverberated with laughter and good cheer. About the room, weather worn faces flourished with smiles. Coffee was served with sandwiches, cookies, and cake. The crescendo of chatter rose, and we were all together, a community, in a little schoolhouse on a vast, northern plain.

A few days later I was in Toronto. From Union Station I took the subway to Bloor Street. Wan-faced passengers packed the car. No one spoke. Thousands of steel-shod souls scurried on and off the concrete platforms at the screeching stations. I smiled at a painted face. It turned away, swinging from the handrail. The car lurched as it squealed around a bend. I grabbed for the rail to steady myself and noticed a smudge on the heel of my hand, picked up by inadvertently touching the city somewhere. Sooty, oily grime it was. I closed my eyes momentarily and smiled as I visualized some good clean mud. I was the only one in the car smiling.

Postscript

Approximately thirty-seven kilometres due east of the town of Nipawin, Saskatchewan's highway fifty-five soars past an inconspicuous sign at the side of the road. The highway is broad, fast, and straight. It invites maximum speed, so it would be easy to miss the little white board with black lettering that says "Battle Heights."

There is nothing else to suggest that this is a place. There is no store, no post office, no garage. Only if for some reason, perhaps nostalgia, you stop at the T-junction, will you notice the remnant of what was once "Bill's Store." It is black with age now and obscured by a barricade of sturdy trees that have grown up in front of it. A little further east, pulled from its original site and tucked in a corner of the lot, sits the old schoolhouse, shuttered and forlorn.

But the land looks good. Broad, flat fields stretch as far as the eye can see. It is rich, northern agricultural land, well tended, and productive.

A mighty embankment and a confident, concrete bridge carry the road high over the Carrot River. Soon, there is another small sign. "Smoky Burn." Here too, the schoolhouse, tattered with age, and neglected, stands as a mute monument to the past, while all around, endless fields of prosperous-looking farmland reach to the horizon. A spacious land. A wilderness subdued.

The farmhouses are modest and compact for the most part, but they are well appointed with furnishings and conveniences. They all have electricity, phones, radio and television, and state of the art indoor plumbing.

The children of the areas are bussed over good roads to attend school in Carrot River. Gone is the spectacle of the student minister struggling against road and weather to keep up with his visiting. There are no more church services and vacation Bible schools in the schoolhouses. There is no store or post office in which to stand about the stove pondering with one's neighbours. Such memories are part of the gradually fading lore of the territory. There really isn't any community left.

Yet there is a community. Scattered though it may be, there is a community of people linked together by memories of those days that time has made sacred. Only a handful of the original settlers are to be found in and around Battle Heights, Smoky Burn, or Papikwan, though several of their sons—the vacation Bible school kids of yesteryear, now married and with families of their own—are farming the land their parents broke and cleared.

Some of the settlers have gone to their eternal rest. Some are living in senior citizens' homes in Carrot River and Nipawin. Others own tidy houses in the same towns. Still others have moved further afield: to Saskatoon, North Battleford, Vancouver Island, or British Columbia's Lower Mainland, there to enjoy their well-earned retirement.

They are scattered but they are a community nevertheless. For they are mystically bound by the pain of having done something difficult with their lives, yet something of great worth. Speak to any of them about the hard times they endured and they will say, "Yeah, there was a lotta hard work. But we had good times, too. A lotta laughs. We sure had some mud back in them days. And the mosquitos was somethin' else. But we had a lotta fun and folks helped each other out. Yeah. It was a purdy good life."

About the Author

Former United Church minister Hugh W. McKervill is the author of *Darby of Bella Bella* and the regional classic, *The Salmon People*. Presently he lives and works in Halifax, Nova Scotia where he is the Atlantic Regional Director for the Canadian Human Rights Commission. In his spare time, McKervill enjoys beekeeping, organic gardening, canoeing, and fishing.